ALL EXPENSES

(Fact meets Fiction)

Helen Ducal

ALL EXPENSES PAID

Copyright © 2011 Helen Ducal

Helen Ducal has asserted her right under the Copyright, Design and Patents Act 1988 to be identified as the author of this work.

This book is a work of fiction, except the parts based on facts.

Acknowledgements.

The town of Martigues

Adrian Paul aka **Highlander**

NRJ. Radio Station

Madonna

Versace

Lalique

Jean Alesi

Elton John

Priscilla. Queen of the Desert. Film

Grace Kelly

Yves Rocher for products and philosophy.

Janet Evanovich. *One for the money.*

Louise L Hay. *You can heal your life.*

Colette. *Cheri and the last of Cheri.*

Golden Girls.

Miami Vice.

The Nightcrawlers. *Push the feeling on.*

ALL EXPENSES PAID

Alpha Romeo.

Renault

VW Golf... Black

Kawasaki

Reviews from Amazon.co.uk kindle edition.

***** **love it**, 26 Aug 2013. by Rosie

What a joy this book is, I loved reading it and couldn't put it down. I love France anyway and this was so funny in places. I loved Betty's character and thought what a wonderful person she was. I would certainly recommend it.

***** **One-off but Hopefully not the Only One**, 17 Aug 2013 by RobertH

What a great read. Sounds like an action packed fun summer, plus a bit. Betty sounds like a fabulous character. I'd love to know if she was the fact or the fiction.

***** **A fab read**, 9 July 2013 by dragon53

I really enjoyed this and thought it was hilarious. she tells the stories with much humour and on some occasions found myself laughing like a fool !!!

*******loved it!** 12 May 2013 by Mrs. P. Phillips "Paulap14" (London UK)

made me laugh at this lovely witty and well written book! really enjoyed this and highly recommended buy and read!

***** **All Expenses Paid - a fun book**, 6 April 2013 by Penny in France

Great fun to read and inspiring if you are over 60 and know you will be heading for Betty's age! Consistently cheerful content.and nice touches about France.

***** **Sheer fun, captured by seamlessly crafted writing**, 19 Feb 2013 by Summer Solstice

I first supposed that the 82 year old Betty, sometimes exhausting and eccentric, might drive her new granny-sitter, Laura, to distraction. Of course, I stood to be wrong but the author had succeeded - I had to read on.

The job specification, Laura's tongue-in-cheek CV and her uncertain balance between excitement and apprehension at looking after the octogenarian are all stamped with a light-hearted and delightfully punchy style.

Pleasantly ensconced in Southern France, Laura's cheeky, sometimes self-effacing view of her new station in life is infectious - the feisty Laura, if heady, then pleasantly endearing.

As Betty 'threw her head back and laughed like a drain' we begin to see that, despite her 82 years, there's no foot in the grave for her either, and she is as vibrant as we could wish; for when Laura and Betty are put together as granny-sitter and granny, a delightfully volatile mix is set alight. Sheer fun, captured by seamlessly crafted writing.

***** **a laugh on each page**, 26 Jan 2013 by **Rosalind E. Boyle**

Just the book for a cold winter day-One to pick up and read again-very unexpected-an enjoyable light read-I wish I could meet the characters.

***** **Grow old gracefully? - Never!!**, 25 April 2012 by **Big Dave**

Just finished reading "All Expenses Paid"...

...not long after beginning to read it!! I couldn't put it down! It's a fantastic read. The big question you're left asking yourself is just how much of that is fact and how much is fiction? Every good work of fiction needs to have you believing that everything that you've read could have happened. I was left convinced that it all did happen, in fact there are some parts that I'd be downright disappointed to find were just Helen's imagination working overtime!!

The world could do with a few more Betty's and I'd love to meet Laura.

Reviews from Amazon.com

***** An entertaining adventure, February 8, 2013 By J Carlberg

Likeable characters and an unpredictable plot made this book an entertaining read. I was sorry to reach the end-I'm hoping for a sequel.

*****Pure Pleasure., December 19, 2012 By bayou grandma (Louisiana) -

As with her other book, a great light read. She is an excellent writer and brings the people and the world(s) in which they live to life for those of us armchair travellers. And without any parading of personal pain to justify living as she does or why she travels abroad - a writing genre of which I am mortally tired. Save me from any more Eat Pray Love.

*****Adorably funny! October 28, 2012 By Jan Janzen -

Well written, with fun characters and at times it had me laughing out loud. I'd love to read more like this!

ALL EXPENSES PAID

* **Not worth the money**, September 21, 2012 By **Patricia Davis** - (REAL NAME)

I enjoy and gravitate towards books about people moving to or visiting other countries. This book was silly and the author seemed quite proud of her sexual experiences while visiting France. I'm glad I hadn't paid a lot of money for it. :(

N.B. Author's note: There is always one isn't there. Thank goodness being silly isn't an actual crime…;-)

*******A favorite kindle purchase!** June 11, 2012 By **PeuAPeu** -

This was one of the most fun and uplifting books I have read in a while. It was so interesting I hardly wanted to put it down. All Expenses Paid had me feeling like I was going through the adventures myself along with these two women. It is definitely a feel-good book. A great read for a rainy day on the sofa.

***** **Fun read**, May 25, 2013 By **lana stephens** (omaha, ne United States) -

I loved the book because the primary character "Betty" is an Octigenarian that prooves you are as young or old as you choose. I had a relationship similar to the two main characters. My friend was Thelma. I was 42 and she was 82 when we met. She taught me that growing old does not mean resigning from life. This would be a fantastic movie!

*****Fun, fun read! March 1, 2013 By **bridgetn**

This book was so much fun to read! I couldn't wait to find out what Betty or Laura were going to do next. It was great because it was fun throughout! I wish I was still reading the book!

*****Sheer fun, captured by seamlessly crafted writing. February 20, 2013 By **Summer Solstice**

I first supposed that the 82 year old Betty, sometimes exhausting and eccentric, might drive her new granny-sitter, Laura, to distraction. Of course, I stood to be wrong but the author had succeeded - I had to read on.
The job specification, Laura's tongue-in-cheek CV and her uncertain balance between excitement and apprehension at looking after the octogenarian are all stamped with a light-hearted and delightfully punchy style.
Pleasantly ensconced in Southern France, Laura's cheeky, sometimes self-effacing view of her new station in life is infectious - the feisty Laura, if heady, then pleasantly endearing.
As Betty 'threw her head back and laughed like a drain' we begin to see that, despite her 82 years, there's no foot in the grave for her either, and she is as vibrant as we could wish; for when Laura and Betty are put together as granny-sitter and granny, a delightfully volatile mix is set alight. Sheer fun, captured by seamlessly crafted writing.

An entertaining adventure, February 8, 2013 By **J Carlberg**

Likeable characters and an unpredictable plot made this book an entertaining read. I was sorry to reach the end-I'm hoping for a sequel.

And before it was available on Amazon. There was authonomy.com and its readers and writers, for which I am truly grateful.

This was written by someone who loves life and knows how to live it. Unlike other British writers who've produced self-aware, often patronising books about life in France, Ducal knows what is meant by joie de vivre and contributes her own take on it. She and Betty delight in what the country has to offer and she uses her writer's gift of observation to identify and select the elements - large and small - that make up its attractive reality. Her voice is clear, direct, inviting as she celebrates her own and Betty's absorption into French ways. It's great fun to read and, at this price, a steal. **W. J. S. Kirton** *The Sparrow Conundrum*.

"**Engaging, fun, unpredictable, fresh, original, silly, and just plain old enjoyable.** Cracking idea and neatly executed. All I need is a deck chair and some sun and I'm sorted!"
ANDREW MORGAN on authonomy.com

"**Part of what makes this book such a tonic** is its constant reminders that life isn't something reserved for the young. I really like the fact that you portray women of a certain age as anything but prim matrons who don't know how to let their hair down! Everything I've read here is suffused with that message." **S. A. STIRLING**

"**This is fun reading, absolutely hilarious**! Who says the English have dry humor. This humor would appeal to anyone. Really lifted my day. The voice is so real and the comedy is side-slapping. My wife made me quit reading it to, come to supper." **STEVE WARD**

"**And they say romance is dead!** Why in the world has no man ever waved a condom at me? This is hysterical. I think I'm in love with Betty. I wish I could hang out with her. She is such a hoot." **MONIQUE O'CONNOR JAMES**

"I'm never sure how much I'll read when I get into a book - well, I figured this would be fun for awhile, and before I realized it I'd read 8 chapters. **FUN? OMG, this is a like a vacation.** Your skills as a writer are evident. This is chick lit plus...plus comedy, plus insight, plus atmosphere."
LIZZI (*Dionysus*)

"**I am already jealous of the freedom from the first few chapters.** Thank you for making me smile and for plunging me so effectively into a different world for the period of time that I was reading, superb writing." **ANDREW WRIGHT** on authonomy.com

"**This funny and charming book should be required reading for all those who anticipate old age with trepidation**. It is a delightful story told with exceptional flair. The characters are beautifully drawn and the dialogue alone should keep a smile on your readers' faces." **KIRKLING**

"**This is a great adventure, and great fun.... and what an alternative life-style**! I think this will attract a huge readership from those wanting to escape the rat-race, and those trapped into it, but who love to read about others braver than them. Come and look after me!" **TONY** on authonomy.com

"**This is so much fun! I love the style**, am flying through chapter after chapter with such ease – can't wipe the smile off my face! Some extremely funny moments, some beautiful descriptions and a unique premise & overall feel to the story. This would put anybody in a good mood! It feels like non-fiction...so

ALL EXPENSES PAID

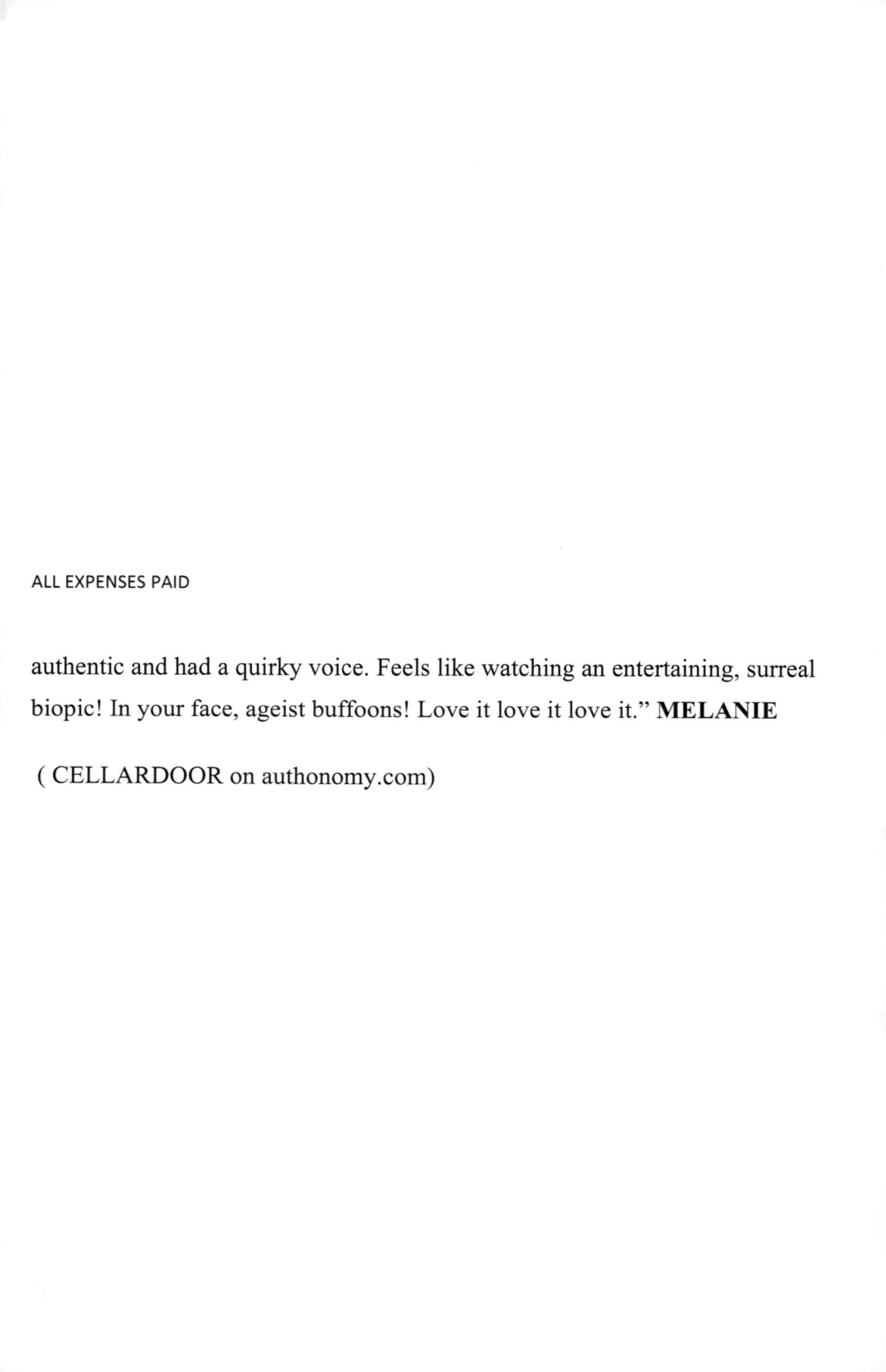

authentic and had a quirky voice. Feels like watching an entertaining, surreal biopic! In your face, ageist buffoons! Love it love it love it." **MELANIE**

(CELLARDOOR on authonomy.com)

Helen Ducal

ALL EXPENSES PAID

For

IPOP

You know who you are.

March 1995

Prologue.

"So why don't you give it a go Laura? It's the best decision I've made in a long time."

This was Grace, my neighbour, newly returned from the Middle East after twelve months as a mother's help and an eighteen thousand pound cheque to show for it.

She had been working, happily enough as a medical secretary and then reading *The Lady* magazine one lunchtime, she saw an advert.

No formal qualifications, just lots of experience, willing to take sole charge, six days per week.

"For goodness sake mother, do it. Think of it as the gap year you never had."

This was Grace's daughter's advice.

"You spent years looking after us. It's like riding a bike."

So that was how it all started. I didn't have any children but I had always worked with people and decided that the other end of the age spectrum would suit me.

"At least they won't move so fast!" agreed Grace.

ALL EXPENSES PAID

Tuesday 27th June 1995

Paradise Found.

Somebody pinch me. Here I am, happily out of bed and it is only seven forty a.m. But it is twenty six degrees in the shade already and I am sitting on the terrace, watching the rhythm of the bright blue water, as it laps against the curved end of the pool. I am sticking my tongue into the froth of my first cappuccino, listening to a lone cicada, stirring behind me.
No really, I am.
 Deirdre and Gerard have just left for work and there is no sign of Betty yet, so I have this world to myself; and this is my job for the next six months.
Julia, I must phone Julia, also known as, the voice of reason. She'll tell me if I'm dreaming.
Okay, it's only six forty in England, better wait a while.
It is amazing that I didn't give up after my first live-in care job with Miss Belcher, pronounced Bel-shah.
But no, I remembered my years of sales training. Never give up; the next call might be The One. Only trouble was, I soon found I was limited to what I could sell.

Three months earlier.

Julia had seen an advert. An up and coming Vacuum Cleaner company required freelance sales agents. Fabulous holidays to be won when you reach your monthly target. Worth a shot I thought.

I had called in to see Julia on my way home after the interview. Julia was receptionist at our local beauty salon. There were no clients needing attention so I sidled up to the desk.

"So how did it go?" Julia said, keeping one eye on the staff room door.

"Well for a man who prided himself on his natural sounding sales scripts. I reckon he cocked up."

"He did, and how did he do that exactly?"

"I couldn't help it; they all looked so bloody serious..."

I continued. "Well we were all sat there, about twelve of us, all paying rapt attention, you unscrew this, attach that there, switch on...bla ...bla... and bingo."

"Sitting, you were all *sitting* there..." Julia could not help herself.I sighed. Julia went to a Grammar school. I did not. We locked eyes. Julia was still with me."Go on," she said. "What did you do?"

"Moi?"

Julia gave me one her looks. The kind that only exasperated best friends can give.

"Well, you know how I'm not always very practical and he *had* only shown us once..."

Now she had her arms folded, bad sign; better hurry up.

"So you couldn't put Humpty back together again, was that it?"

"Oh I did but apparently not the right way round, but it did seem to fit."

"And you failed the interview over one attempt?"

"Erm, no, not exactly, you see I was about to switch on, thinking I'd got it right, when Mr-oh-so-smarmy- Area Manager says. "Stop. Think. Do you want to blow or suck?"

"Oh God." Julia had her hands over her eyes. "And you said?"

"Shouldn't you at least take me out to dinner first?"

Julia's jaw line gave her away. She was laughing. "You're hopeless."

With that, the phone rang. I nodded my departure and Julia swallowed hard to regain her composure before answering the phone.

****

And then four days later, Julia rang to ask if it would be okay to bring Doris to my, leaving-the country-do. Julia would drop her off before we went clubbing... if we had the energy. Doris is Julia's mother in law. At seventy nine, I thought we were going to be seriously restricted in our conversation. Julia assured me I would be pleasantly surprised. We had decided to go for a drink at our unlikely favourite hideaway; the bar of a faceless hotel but conveniently placed a mile and a half from each of us. Fridays were always quiet, until we arrived. All the business clients had scarpered back to their weekend lives. We would have one drink each and then just keep topping up with tonic or dry ginger. We did not need alcohol to lift our spirits. I was having an in depth discussion with a couple of the female bar staff about whether size does matter, when Julia and Doris joined us.

"Men?" asked Julia looking at the three of us.

"No, last Saturday's football results." I suggested.

"Oh me god, I might as well go home then." This was Doris, a mass of white hair, smelling of lily of the valley and a ring on every finger.

"Don't worry Ma, they're only kidding. So, what were you talking about?"

Drinks appeared as if by magic. Julia must have ordered them on her way in. The young barman, tall, blonde and clean cut, eyed us all with trepidation.

"Nuts?" enquired Julia. We all nodded. "Large mixed, salted. Thanks."

"So, tonight's topic of conversation...hmm?"

I had already checked and Julia said her mother in law was as broad minded as the rest of us.

"Size versus technique." I offered.

We all blinked at Doris as she said, "Well, you do want it to touch the sides."

The ice was well and truly broken. The nuts arrived courtesy of one of the regular barmen.

"Thanks Ben," we said in unison.

The new recruit was at the far end of the bar and had been polishing the same glass for the last ten minutes.

"He's new, he's young." Ben nodded at the bar, "Be gentle with him ladies."

ALL EXPENSES PAID

****

But there was no ice here. It was the start of the fourth day since I had left the girls behind and so much had happened already. I checked my watch, shaking it loose to make sure the white line was still there. Six sessions on the sun bed had paid off.

Where had the last hour gone? Eight forty. I could not wait any longer.

"Julia, it's me...I know I'm sorry it's so early...what? No nothing's wrong...Oh is that your pager...Okay speak to you tonight."

I put the white, banana shaped, cordless phone down on the white painted wrought iron table. It rocked back and forth. I was in a trance. Could this be any different from my first live-in care job...?

Tuesday 11th April.

The advert and my escape to the sun.

I am one of life's sprinters not a long distance runner.

So here I am on my first assignment. Assignment. Thoughts of phone boxes... message will self destruct...should you decide to accept. Mission Impossible? Surely not.

I pulled into the drive; I looked across at the passenger seat and the latest copy of *The Lady* magazine sticking out of my overstuffed, brown, pseudo-leather handbag. Oh well, if this was a nightmare at least I could start looking for the next job straightaway. I had agreed to look after *this* lady for three weeks. Jonathan, the nephew had been insistent that his aunt, albeit reluctant to have live in help was nonetheless, no bother. She was very independent and only needed someone there, just in case. Note to anyone considering a career in care work there is a deep dark chasm between need and want, as I was soon to find out.

The house was a thirties semi, in rural Warwickshire. So far; so good. I looked down at my wrist and my new watch; a crazy acquisition, a moment of madness. A silver bracelet inlaid with marquisates, and a tiny silver dolphin either side of the face. It wasn't so much that I liked it, I was drawn to it. I had to have it. I didn't need it but I wanted it. Unlike Aunt- no bother- Joan, who needed help but didn't want it.

ALL EXPENSES PAID

It was eleven thirty five a.m. time I went in and relieved the present carer, who had sounded very nice on the phone. The porch door was open. A regiment of potted geraniums lined the adjoining garage wall. Very neat and tidy. Just as well she could not see the inside of my car. I was not going to be too far from home, but not near enough to pop back, so I had brought, well, everything bar the kitchen sink. One bag held six books. I reckoned on reading two a week. I mean, she had a cleaner twice a week and a gardener, I only had to shop and cook. I had it all planned, even written out sample menus, to save time. Oh well, this is it.

****

Four hours later, on my two hour break, I am down the road in the phone box.

"Hi Julia, it's me. I've just seen a great ad for a job in the South of France!"

"Oh yes..."

"No really I have. It's in this week's *Lady* Magazine. Listen. 6 months in the South of France, granny sitting, while family travels. Separate en-suite accommodation, own TV and use of family car. Ideally 40+, male or female and non smoker. Interviews London in April. Start June. Please phone after 8pm. It's a French number."

"Blimey. Just want *one* person do they?"

"Afraid so. What do you think?"

"What do you mean, what do I think? Phone them for God's sake."

"Are you sure. I could be away six months and what about all my stuff that I am going to put in your spare room?"

Julia interrupted. "Well you can always pay rent if it will make you feel any happier."

"Well, um, I could manage..."

"Only kidding, idiot. You'd do the same for me wouldn't you?"

It was more of a statement than a question. Julia and I went back a long way. We were more like sisters, sisters with different parents that is. Julia is tall, has long dark wavy hair and is big boned (her expression). I am short with a blonde bob and can wear children's jewellery. We'd met back in the dark ages at hairdressing college. I practised putting up her long hair, backcombed to infinity and with enough grips to set off the metal detectors at Heathrow. She put me through agony, pulling strands of hair through a rubber highlight cap with a number three crochet hook. We shopped at Biba and thought Vidal Sassoon was God. She wanted to be small and slim. I desperately wanted her cleavage (well not hers but a similar one of my own). We decided at seventeen that if any man wanted the perfect woman she was right here, only he would have to have the two of us. We had both got married three years later, within two months of each other. Julia was my bridesmaid; I was her 'old maid' of honour. She still had her husband; mine had wandered off years ago. If she had not been my best friend I could have been quite envious. She seemed to have the best of worlds, a nice big house, a part-time job as a receptionist at the local salon and a husband who was away for weeks at a time. Perfect.

Julia brought me out of my reverie.

"How's it going there anyway?"

"Don't ask."

"That bad?"

"Worse. She looks at me as though I have been cleaning drains for a living and have brought the smell with me. Think she'd charge me for the air I was breathing if she could find a way."

"Better make sure it's not her twin sister in the South of France then."

"God forbid!"

"Did the last carer give you any useful tips?"

"Ah..."

"Uh-oh. What ah?"

"Well, you know how I really, really try, never to assume?"

No comment from Julia, just a snigger. So I continued.

" I arrived early, went round the back of the house and into the kitchen as instructed and explained to the small white haired lady sitting at the kitchen table that I just had get some things from the car and I'd be right back to get lunch started."

"And she turned out to be the next door neighbour? Or no, don't tell me you were in the wrong house?"

"No Julia, I was not in the wrong house but honestly if you had seen her, you..."

"Oh no."

"Yep, when I went back in, the aforementioned white haired lady was still sitting at the table, when the kitchen door opens and in walks Miss Belcher. The seated geriatric waves her hand towards the clearly even older white haired lady and says, with what can only be described as disdain. 'And *this* is Miss Belcher. The lady you will be looking after.' Only she pronounced it Belshah. Don't you know."

"Great start then."

"Yeah well, she liked her lemon meringue pie. Anyway I'd better go; she'll be wanting her afternoon cup of tea. I'll phone you tomorrow after I've rung about the job, okay?"

"Okay sweet pea."

"Very funny dragonfly."

We had not used our old nicknames for ages. They sounded even more absurd as we got older. Julia had called me sweet pea one day when she had given me a friendly shove and I had fallen over. Imagine sweet peas without the canes and string. Julia's name evolved from her arms always flapping about when trying to explain something.

"By the way, Laura, why don't you give me the number where you're working and I'll phone you, if she won't let you call me?"

"Ha! Tried that. She said I couldn't receive calls as it would tie up her line."

"Oh boy. Good luck with the frog job."

Julia always likes to wind me up about my passion for all things French but today I did not care. I just wanted to get through the next three weeks with my sanity and reputation as a kind and considerate carer intact. I phoned the number in France. There was an answering machine so I left a message, giving Aunt

Sourpuss' number, explaining that the call would have to be between four thirty and nine thirty pm and that it would have to be very brief.

I got back into the house at ten past four. No signs of movement in the living room. Good; time to put the kettle on. A gilt edged tray had been left on the table, set out precisely for afternoon tea. Different china, even a different teapot was used in the afternoons. A handwritten note was alongside the kettle. One spoonful of Darjeeling and a slice of lemon, on a saucer. Cube sugar in silver sugar bowl and silver tongs in the left hand cutlery drawer. At twenty past four I delivered the tray. Madam Belcher was watching the snooker. She patted the neatly tied bow of her cream silk M and S blouse, with her left hand. She pointed with her right hand to indicate the nest of tables at the side of her chair. Possibly a sign of irritation?

She glanced at the tray, her nostrils twitching. "Strainer," she sighed.

Ah, yes, loose tea, strainer required. I charged back into the kitchen like a Retriever intent on pleasing its master. After opening three cupboards and two drawers, voila, silver tea strainer complete with stand.

I produced it with a smile. I was rewarded with. "Supper at six thirty."

Her pale grey eyes never left the screen. She replaced her hands on her lap, disturbing the lie of her navy box pleat skirt, which nudged her ankles. Her navy lace up shoes would be replaced by slippers in time for the six o clock news. I retreated to the kitchen. I know my place. I made myself a cup of tea. An Earl Grey tea bag, in a mug and sat down on a stool to read the notes left by the previous carer. When the phone rang twenty minutes later I knocked over my mug and the dregs of my tea. Thank goodness for Formica but I didn't stop to mop up in case the call was my salvation. I need not have rushed. I just had my hand on the living room door, when I heard.

"No. No, I'm all alone. Jonathan is away on business but he is only my nephew. How is your son doing these days?"

I was so tempted to go in and say, loudly, 'Oh sorry, just wanted to see if your tea was to your liking and if you'd like another slice of cake?' or 'My god, tell me, when did I become invisible?'

But, I refrained.

The next call came at six twenty. I was urging a shepherd's pie to brown under the grill. It was already hot but looked so anaemic. I heard, "I'm sorry you must have the wrong number."

Uh-oh. I quickly removed the grill pan from under the grill and put it on the draining board and shot into the living room. Too late, she had already replaced the receiver.

"Was it someone asking for Laura?" I tried to sound casual.

"Why, is that you?" She looked incredulous; perhaps I was not supposed to have a name.

"Yes. I'm sorry but it's about my next job, and I did phone them from the phone box this afternoon and I did explain that it would have to be a very quick call."

"You gave someone, a stranger... my number?"

For some reason, 'my number' sounded like Lady Bracknell saying, my handbag. Now, I did not actually laugh but my face has a mind of its own, apparently, and Lady Belcher was not amused. The phone rang again. I smiled, weakly. "Please. It will only take a minute, then I will arrange a time for tomorrow, at the phone box."

She nodded. If she pinched her mouth in any harder she was at serious risk of resembling the knot at the end of a balloon. I was handed the receiver as Madam Belcher glanced at the grandfather clock in the corner of the room, six twenty six p.m. I explained the situation to my potential employer, who sounded sympathetic. We agreed I would find a fax machine; the number was the same she assured me. I replaced the receiver. With a nod and a smile, which was now, getting no further than my mouth, I retreated to the kitchen as the grandfather clock chimed the half hour. The shepherd's pie, pale as ever, would have to do. Carrots and peas at least gave some colour. I tried to dismiss any thoughts of moules et frites as I scooped out the traditional fare. Aunt Joan's preferred mode of staying alive. At least I had remembered to warm the Pyrex, kitchen use only, plates.

The next twenty one days passed peacefully enough once I discovered that nothing I did was quite good enough. I made her bed. Hospital corners, no less. Aunt- quite –a-lot-of-bother-Joan felt the need to verify this by stripping the bed, just to check. I also learned that there are three tins with three kinds of biscuits. Large red round tin, best shortbread and ginger thins for hers and bridge players mouths only. Square blue tin, digestives and bourbons for family visitors. White Tupperware container with rich tea for the help (that will be me) and the gardener. The cleaner has coffee at the end of her shift but no biscuits. Presumably too much of a crumb hazard?

And when I felt the time dragging I envisaged my upcoming interview with a Frenchman in Brixton. I had faxed my CV and got a reply a week later. It was a start. Mental note to self. Make sure you have the right person before you start blathering in French, he may just be the plumber who happens to answer the door. But I needn't have worried. I mean there is French and then there is...Bonjour!

ALL EXPENSES PAID

Saturday 27th May.

The Interview. A Frenchman in Brixton.

Never been here before. Rows of terraced houses, three storey ones, mostly freshly painted in bright colours. Gardens replaced by something solid for the 2cv or Nova to stand on. Curtains; different at all the windows, bedsits maybe. English suburbia.

I smoothed down my cream linen trouser suit, to absolutely no effect. So comfortable, so crumpled. I made sure, however, that my favourite Azur blue silk scarf was perfectly knotted through a loop, French style. I checked my crazy new watch. Ten minutes late. Perfect. The French do not do timing to the minute, like the Brits. Fortunately, I must have French genes.

I pressed the bell and a muted buzz was immediately followed by the door opening. Mmm...dark, not too closely shaven, fine tortoiseshell rimmed glasses and an accent to die for. At last, my employer. Shame he was going to be away.

"A glass of wine?" he offered before we were barely inside.

Now I knew he was French.

"My wife is English of course and she speaks. ..er...very good French but my mother in law, she is not keen to learn the language, so we need someone to look after her while we are going away."

I grabbed at the large glass of red wine that he had placed in front of me on the low coffee table, and took a large gulp. It was twenty minutes past twelve and on an empty stomach I was hoping it would do the trick. Thank god I had come by train. The thing is my French improves greatly with the aid of red wine, well, any alcohol really; as to why? Je ne sais pas.

Gerard began to speak in French. He had warned me previously, on the phone, that he would.

'alf the interview will be en Francais, d'accord?

Oui, oui,' I had enthused. Oh, there goes my doorbell, must dash, see you on Saturday, a bientot.

So there I was, bemused by his long slender fingers wrapped around that sheer bulbous glass of wine. His tan, I was sure, would be even. Just enough dark hair on his knuckles to show a good circulation of testosterone, without having a hairy back. The index finger of his right hand gently nudged his glasses back up his slender nose and into place as he stared at me with palest green eyes. His pale lemon cashmere (probably) jumper was casually draped around his shoulders and began to slide. A matching short sleeved tee shirt complete with collar was tucked into the waistband of his dark brown designer jeans. Could he be any more French? I smiled as he titled his head to one side.

He was waiting for an answer.

Question, question, what the hell had he asked me?

I was too busy playing 'me, English wife' to listen properly. Time for the charm offensive.

"Oh I'm sorry. Could you repeat the question. It's just, well, oh, how can I say it?"

"Oui?"

"Well, it's silly I know, but it's just your wonderful accent...I erm...lost concentration."

The warmth from the red wine apparently found its way back up to his neck and then crept around his jaw line before he spoke again.

"Ah yes well. We will continue in English." He cleared his throat.

A frog, I wondered? I later found out that the French equivalent is 'le chat' or a cat.

A fully ripened brie was oozing its way to the edge of the plate, along with pate and ever so crusty bread which Gerard brought to the coffee table at twelve thirty.

"But of course we normally have zee proper meal at midday, but I have two more peoples to interview, so time, you know?"

I wondered if they would all get the red wine treatment.
I was not worried; with a bit of luck he might not even be able to focus on the last one.
We shook hands on the doorstep.
There was a moment's pause as we both considered the usual Gallic cheek to cheek...and decided against it.

"Deirdre, she will call you. Au revoir."

****

Wednesday 7th June.

The phone rang and I picked it up on the second ring. I was just going up to the village shop. I had run out of masking tape. I glanced at the three piles of boxes. Keep, throw, don't know. You can guess which pile was the highest.

"Sorry it's taken so long. Gerard says you're just perfect."

Ah Deirdre's dulcet tones. For what I wondered?

"We were wondering... if you wouldn't mind driving, only we've had problems with the car. We'd pay all your expenses, of course. Think of it as a little holiday. See some of France on the way. But don't fall in love with anywhere else, will you, or get another job? Can you start at the end of June, as we planned? It's just twenty days away. Oh dear. Do hope you're going say yes."

I could have gone off and made a cup of tea in the time it had taken her to ask one question, never mind just say yes.

So I began. "Well, there is one thing..."

"Oh dear, oh dear, I knew we should have phoned you sooner, what can I say?"

Lots, apparently.

"Madam Moulin, if I may just interrupt?"

"Oh, yes, yes, sorry. Do go on."

"Yes I can come," I paused.

I swear I heard her mouth open and then close.

I continued. "However…"

I love this word; it has a feeling of power about it…driving seat and all that. "I will need the money in advance."

"Of course, of course, how much is it, have you worked it out?"

Her oxygen supply temporarily suspended I jumped in.

"Well no actually, you've only just offered me the job, so I…"

"Oh of course my dear, how silly of me. Now just you phone me back when you have it all worked out and don't forget to allow for meals on the way and petrol and then there's the peage; I'm sure you know that means tolls, don't you, if you've travelled in France before, and then there'll be your hotel overnight, not five star I'm afraid, it'll have to be a chambre d'hotel or something similar and have you checked your insurance; oh no silly me, you didn't know you'd get the job, silly me," she stopped. "Are you still there?"

This time I had put her on speaker phone. I had made the tea, flicked through the local paper, waved to my neighbour who was out walking the dog and was just getting the milk out of the fridge so I replied.

"Yes, I'm here."

"Oh good, thought we'd been cut off." She laughs hysterically.

I wondered if she had shares in France Telecom, perhaps I should suggest it.

"Oh and do call me Charlene. Just between us…"

Why, I wondered would I want to do that. A nice English girl called Charlene, especially when the letter I had received had been headed, Gerard and Deirdre Moulin.

"I know, you're wondering about my name. I wanted to change it in the eighties. I just adored Dallas, and Deirdre, well it's just too close to dreary, don't you think? Mother just calls me D. Gerry calls me all sorts of things. The French are soo romantic don't you think? He told me you liked his accent. Isn't it to die for?"

This woman is, well, unique, can't think of another word for her...I was intrigued, what did she look like, she sounded so much older than him. And how the hell did she manage a catch like Gerard. She was obviously waiting for a reply.

"Yes, I've always thought a French accent was charming." I suggested carefully, although I am not sure even if I said, *Yeah, he can give me one any time.* She would have done anything but laugh. Best not to push my luck though. Julia had been priming me.

"Indeed." Deirdre pauses. I'm sure there is more. "Oh and Laura."

"Yes, erm, Charlene?"

"You know the advert said own TV?"

I nodded and then realised we were not using a video phone. "Yes," I said cautiously.

"Well of course I should have checked it. The advert I mean. Gerard wrote it you see."

I gently opened my front door and reached round to the door bell. I had to press it twice before it rang. I needn't have bothered. Either Deirdre didn't hear it or chose not to.

"Deir, I mean Charlene. I have to go; there is someone at my door."

"Oh, yes, sorry. Off you go then..."

"Um, the television. You were saying something about..?"

"Oh gosh, yes. What Gerard really meant to say was. You will have to bring your own TV, we don't have one, you see...at all."

And then my doorbell really did ring. It was Grace my next door neighbour. All this was her fault. I nodded and smiled at Grace as I opened the door.

I told Deirdre not to worry and that I would call her back once I had worked out my route and expenses.

****

Thursday 22nd June.

I was sad to be leaving my draughty old cottage but the farmer wanted it back. He had given me three months notice, so I was prepared. He was going to convert it into three small flats. Ugh. I was glad I wasn't going to be around to see it. The end of the twentieth century. Character replaced by commercialism. It took five trips in my car to take all my stuff to Julia's. I felt our friendship stretched almost to the limit as we squeezed ourselves around piles of boxes and out the door of Julia's ...box room.

I bit my lip and Julia rolled her eyes. We would survive.

Saturday 24th June.

Am I nearly there yet?

I arrived at my half way destination, Tournus, in time to find a room for the night and a meal.

Although it was a Saturday evening, it was June and I thought it would be easy but I was mindful of getting somewhere before seven pm and the serious business of the evening meal began. I needed a secure car park as there was no way I could empty my car. I had my overnight bag on the floor, of the passenger side. I headed for centre-ville and found a wonderful meandering small town with twin churches, cobbled streets and a gently flowing river. What had Deirdre said about not falling in love with anywhere en-route? As it turned out I was spoilt for choice. This town and nearby Cluny I would return to, in years to come.

I had already learned not to judge hotels or restaurants in France by their facades; a shabby chic exterior could contain a Michelin star chef. Once I had found my room I quickly splashed some water on my face and headed downstairs. I was aware that small hotels expect their clients to eat in their dining rooms. I really wanted to explore the town before dark but I also wanted to play by 'the rules'.

By eight p.m. the oak panelled dining room was humming with the gentle chatter of contented customers. Not unusually, there was a set menu. No choice. I was not disappointed. A salad for starters. Think salad niçoise without the tuna. Then quail cooked with honey and mustard, endive and sauté potatoes.

There was a choice of dessert. Crème brulée or tart aux pommes. I had the tart. I marvelled at the delicate slices of apple and how carefully they had been arranged to overlap with perfect symmetry. I opted for decaffeinated coffee. Shattered but equally excited, usually meant a sleepless night. However much I tried the 'now go to sleep or Father Christmas won't come' routine that had been instilled in me, as a child... I do not know why I bothered. It did not work then, so why now?

I was surprised to see the other diners appeared to be local, greeting each other politely with the customary, bonsoir and a slight nod of the head. I was accorded polite glances but no bonsoirs. Draining the tiny coffee cup I decided to take a quick tour of the town. Le patron was back behind the reception desk when I left the dining room so I asked for a map of the town. He produced an A4 sheet of paper. A photocopy. With a red pen he silently circled a spot on the bottom right hand corner of the very hazy map. The photocopier needed an ink refill. My French didn't run to this. So I just thanked him and asked if the red spot was...Vous êtes ici? He assured me with a wry smile that it was and then started to proclaim something of apparent great importance. I had no idea what he was saying. He sighed. He waved his arms at the door. He pointed to the ceiling. He did not actually say, les Anglais, but...

The moment was saved by a very smart elderly gentleman sporting a handlebar moustache that defied gravity and was pointing east-west, as if indicating where his ears were. Monsieur le patron sprang on him. "Ah Claude. Vous parlez anglais?"

Claude nodded the affirmative. As he listened to the hotelier, Claude smiled and nodded once more. The moustache never wavered. Claude turned to me and said. "Mademoiselle, the hotel is locked at ten p.m."

He glanced up at the grandfather clock by the fireplace. It was ten minutes past nine. Monsieur le patron had added something else. It was hard to believe that, that was all he had said. Maybe Claude was being, how shall I say, diplomatic?

"Ah, oui. There is no bell for the night." Claude looked at me hoping to see recognition in my tired eyes.

I nodded feverently and promised to be back by nine forty five, after a quick walk, as I had been in the car since Calais, I was in need of some fresh air, help me sleep, you see? Claude did see. He nodded. Monsieur le patron raised eyebrows were placated by Claude, who spoke assuredly. "Oui, elle comprend."

I thanked Claude for his help and nodded to Monsieur le patron. He sighed.

Just as I had thought earlier, Tournus was a place to come back to but as soon as the fresh air hit me I felt all the tiredness that had been cowering under my enthusiasm, get the better of me. I walked quickly to the top of the hill in time to see the twin church towers disappear into a pink and grey sky. I was back in my room by nine thirty. I had a long day ahead tomorrow, I needed sleep and it came as soon as my head hit the pillow.

By eleven p.m. I was wide awake, again. I could hardly pop and make some cocoa so I had two other options that usually work when I cannot get back to sleep. Read or write. Or better still dictate my journey, so far. This small machine had become a good friend of late especially when I was driving so much. I found if I put the dictaphone on my lap (absolutely no need for comments here, thank you) and pressed record I could keep a diary of my journey.

It was so quiet in this hotel and I did not know if anyone was next door so I disappeared underneath the sheet and quilt to add my final thoughts of the day. I had promised Julia I would write regularly. I had a moment of déjà vu, as the gentle whirring of the tape machine and the tiny red glow took me back to school days (or nights) and my transistor tuned to radio Luxembourg. Ovaltine for the ears, Kenny Everet called it. Ah, bless him. I rewound the tape and started dictating my first letter to Julia.

Dear Julia,

I know I've only been gone twenty four hours but I just had to write and tell you what's happened already. Okay, so I got down to Dover for the 6 a.m. ferry, no problem. And there it was, my first French lorry and I'm still at the dock, with its very own French lorry driver leaning up against his sixteen wheeler, reading the A-Z of Great Britain. Do they have the heat on full blast in those cabs or was the short sleeved white t-shirt stretched over Desperate Dan forearms just showing off?

Anyway, you know me, brilliant with a map and fluent in French, so over I went.

"Quelle est le problème monsieur?" I could tell he was impressed. However his answer was a little quicker than my tired brain could cope with, so I did what the French always do to me when they don't know the answer. I simply nodded enthusiastically, said Oui, two or three times until he folded his map and climbed back into his cab.

I'm sure he'll like Nottingham once he gets used to the accent.

It wasn't until I got back into the car that I remembered I had been driving in 'comfort mode'. I looked down. Sure enough my jeans zip was half way down and I was still wearing my 'not even to be buried in' trainers. So much for Le chic Anglaise.

I took your advice and stayed in the car until I was parked on the car deck. If I didn't see the sea I wouldn't know it was there. It's all in my imagination. The sign for Dover on the M2 does not have an uneasy swell about it. Must be a trick of the light. I mean what's there to be nervous about? You can't exactly get off at the wrong stop. It's Calais and then point due south.

I'm not on a huge boat about to sail across the busiest shipping lane in the world. I'm just going into this restaurant to have breakfast. The plate is not going to start sliding towards the raised lip around the edge of the table. I will sit in the middle. I will not look out of the windows, I mean portholes. I'll be fine. Your words kept coming back to me.

Okay, anything else you told me to do? Oh yes stop thinking about it. Buy a paper, read everyone's stars. Concentrate. I drove onto the car deck and locked the car. Then I remembered I have to leave it in first gear, which was fine because it gave me time to find a piece of paper and write down my location.

Car Deck P, near the wide flat end, orange stairs. So that's P for puke, orange as in juice, wide and flat. The shape of my mouth as I throw up!

My mind has a mind of its own and a bizarre sense of humour. Distractions, that's what I need.

I followed the clattering human hoards up the steep metal steps to the main passenger decks. Just enough time for breakfast and I'll be there. No problem. And there wasn't. I don't know what you were worrying about?

It was about 8.30 when I arrived in Calais. I know you like planning where you're going to stop but I prefer to go with the flow. I don't know how you know when you're going to feel tired, hungry, need a pee, or all three. So I set off with

ALL EXPENSES PAID

a tank full of English petrol, stomach full of bacon, eggs, sausage, tomato, toast and coffee.

I didn't stop until about 10.30, but it was worth it.

****

At this point I hit the pause button. I heard the muffled boing of the grandfather clock downstairs.
 Midnight. Time to sleep. No more musings. The rest could wait. I was hardly going to forget.
I clicked the stop button and it seemed to resound around the room. Sorry, I whispered from under my bedclothes. Happily no-one replied. I checked, again, that my alarm was still set for seven thirty am. I needn't have worried. Have you ever tried to sleep through the sound of coffee being freshly ground? Not to mention the aroma wafting up the stairs at seven a.m.

Sunday 25th June.

I set off at eight a.m. It was a beautiful bright morning. It seemed a pity to take the auto route but I still had a long way to go and I wanted to get to my destination and new home as soon as possible. I clicked the milometer to 0. I found a suitable radio station, playing Madonna's *Holiday*. I waited until I was out of the town before turning it up, full blast. I was having a grown up *Famous Five* adventure. At least I reckoned that was the reason for my silly grin reflected in the rear view mirror as I glanced up, ready to put Beryl (my long suffering, yellow and black, roll top, Renault 5) through her paces.

I had been reading about these new fangled motorway hotels. The automated kind. Apparently there were staff during the day but at night, after nine p.m. you 'let yourself in' with a credit card. Hmm. I was sure the system worked but, credit cards, instructions in French, machines...Not wanting to test my French too much, I arrived at the F1 hotel in time to be welcomed by a human, with half an hour to spare. I pulled into the car park at the Valence junction. This would leave me just 220 kms for tomorrow morning.

This F1 was brand new and therefore clean but not the place for anything other than, getting your head down. Think; over large porta-cabin. I just hoped the Mistral never reached this far, as it felt as though the whole place might blow over. I asked for a room by the car park. There was no way I could empty the car. Did I mention it was full to the roof, with my portable television /video on the passenger seat?

If anyone tried to take my car, at least I would hear them and I could wave. Of course having a room adjacent to the car park meant that late night arrivals would shine their lights into my room. Genius. Ah well. The double bed with a bunk bed above it was firm, probably too firm for a decent night's sleep. The room was painted cream with a bright red, built-in chrome dressing table. For the most part I am very French in my habits, bar one. Must have a cup of tea, available, somehow. So, there I was with my mini kettle and adaptor plug, mug, tea bags and sugar. I would have to forgo the milk.

The only socket was jammed up against the bedpost and designed naturally to take a French plug. Sadly, by the time I had plugged the kettle into the adaptor it wouldn't fit in the socket. Funny how desperately you need a cuppa, when you can't have one. So, I went into the corridor in search of a vending machine that I had spotted on my way in. Now, I had read enough about these F1 hotels and knew that they operated on pin-code system for all the doors. No keys required but you do need to remember your number. I was not going to get caught out, so I wrote the number down and put it in my pocket. The toilets and showers were also along the corridor but I couldn't be bothered with a proper wash tonight, so I just had a pee, careful to make sure the bit of paper with my number on it, did not fall down the loo. I found the vending machine and opted for decaffeinated coffee.

Back safely in my room, I noted that Beryl was outside my window, just as I had left her. Her contents covered with various rugs. Nothing to see...move along please! Don't leave valuables on show in your car. Sensible police advice but when you are basically moving house...well, what can you do?

There were no curtains just a roller blind, so I pulled it down and hooked the loop securely at the bottom. I was soon aware of my dubious choice of room as car after car arrived and lit up my room, casting comical shadows on the walls. There was a small halogen light over the bed for reading (see, civilised) so I put that on as I wasn't too sure how thick the blind was. It was a very mild night, so I pulled out a thin cotton night shirt, from my overnight bag and laid it on the bed. I ran some warm water in the basin, not too much or the sound would make me want to pee again and I didn't want to venture into the corridor until breakfast time when the humans returned. I threw my jeans, tee shirt, bra and pants across the other side of the bed. Because I could. No one saying...don't put it down, put it away. Great advice, which I follow, occasionally.

So, naked as a jaybird I went over to the basin. The blind was a fairly good fit to the window, quite snug in fact. There had been no lights or sounds for a few moments so I peeked outside. I only nudged the side of the blind but it shot upwards free from its hook at the bottom. As I reached up to grab the hook on the bottom of the blind...naturally at that moment a 4x4 drives into the car-park, filling my room with more light than a west end stage.

I dropped down onto the floor like something out of a bad cop show. My night shirt was not within reach and the only towel provided would cover one nipple, at a push. I waited for the 4x4 occupants to disembark before moving. I crawled round to the bottom of the bed and grabbed my night shirt. The one with Elmo's head on it. I switched off the light over the bed and tried to stretch up to retrieve the blind. It had shot up with such force; it was higher up than when I arrived.

There was a three legged metal, bright red stool. If I stood on this...Oh, crikey, another car. Headlights did a tour of my room. I was staying in Colditz! This car seemed to have endless occupants. I could hear raised voices coming from the entrance. Tired travellers, credit cards, French instructions, machines...

Finally I got the blind back in situ, i.e. covering the window but now I saw my real problem. The loop that held it in place was broken and so would not stay down. Now to try and find something to fix it I would have to let it go. I tried to grab some coat-hangers but they were out of reach. They would at least slow down the ascent but then might tear the material. Hey ho. I let it go. I might

ALL EXPENSES PAID

have been chucked out of the brownies but I still lived by the 'be prepared' motto. Or was that the scouts?

What seemed like forever but was probably fifteen minutes later and I had managed to anchor the blind with two intertwined elastic bands. I just hoped they would hold until morning. I clambered into bed and set the alarm on my travel clock. The last car arrived at three fifteen. I slept until six thirty when the staff began arriving. They were not noisy but the smell of freshly baked croissants and chug of the coffee machine announced the start of another day.

In a few hours I would meet Betty. I just hoped that I wouldn't be too much for her. Miss Belcher of course had insisted that I was not suited to this line of work. Far too bubbly. Old people want a quiet life and I would do well to remember that.

But how exciting, six months in the South of France and all expenses paid. I couldn't wait to get started.

Monday 26th June.

Arrival. Betty and her stroke of genius.

"We think Mother may have had another slight stroke since we last spoke; so we'll need you to keep an extra eye on her." Deirdre pronounced as she flung open my driver's door. So English. Not even a Bonjour or Hello. I had just pulled up by the terrace of my new home. The house is a 60's detached villa. Not quite the Provencal mas I had envisaged, but it was huge and placed squarely in a dry and dusty, neglected garden. Four giant pines provided welcome shade but I already had my eye on the two apricot trees nestling against a west wall. How lovely. The possibility to pluck your pudding straight from the tree. I winced at my alliteration.

We had only spoken yesterday afternoon, so I wondered if the stress of her family leaving and having some strange woman move in; could be the cause of this latest problem? I know I was nervous, so I was sure Betty must be.
I turned the key in the ignition and patted Beryl on the dashboard, muttering a silent thank you. My car's engine shuddered to a halt, as if it was hard to believe it was allowed to stop.
"Deirdre," I stated, momentarily closing my eyes, recognising the voice.

Did the body fit the voice? No, it did not. I thought Deirdre would be glamorous, in an upper class English kind of way. Expensively tailored trousers, leather loafers, hundred percent cotton tee shirts and pearl earrings. I glanced behind Deirdre as Gerard's voice announced. "Ah Laura. She is 'ere."

Gerard appeared and I realised that he was wearing what I thought Deirdre would look like, minus the pearl earrings. Next came Mother a diminutive five foot nothing, ablaze with that colourful, good fake jewellery that you can get these days. She walked slowly, with a very slight stoop and a crooked smile. She took Gerard's arm as he helped her down the three stone steps from the terrace, across the parched and brittle grass, to stand beside Deirdre. I peered out at them all. I smiled.

"Bonjour Laura et Bienvenu."

"Merci Gerard. Hello Betty."

Betty was positioned just behind and between her daughter and son-in-law.

"So, as I say...do you think you will be able to cope? It was only a mini stroke, a TAI, I think they call it?"

At the mention of a stroke, Betty obligingly lolloped slightly to the right, whilst managing to wink at me at the same time.
How I did not laugh, I will never know.
Deirdre was continuing her list of updated instructions, and I had not even got out of the car; not offered any refreshment; I was getting annoyed.
"Our doctor does speak English, so if you have any problems, any problems at all..."

Gerard gave a slight cough into the back of his hand. I raised my eyes to his. He shrugged.
My attention span was darting from Betty's, otherwise known as Mother, perfectly puce lips, imitating her daughter's speech, to the swimming pool cover, as it ebbed and flowed, caught up with the light breeze.
Deirdre followed my gaze. "Ah yes."

Her voice rose, two very unnecessary octaves.

"We've decided to cover the pool whilst we're away; mother, her condition and all that, sure you understand."

Oh yes, sure. I have just driven eight hundred miles to a job in the south of France. It is June, it is twenty eight degrees and you declare the pool out of bounds, what could be more understandable? At which point Betty surpassed herself by sticking her middle, precisely manicured, finger in the air, behind her daughter's back.

"Deirdre darling, do let the poor girl at least come and sit down and recover from her journey. How about some tea?"

Betty had resumed the sprightly but frail mother-in-law as described by Gerard at the interview. She obviously had them all fooled.

"Of course. What was I thinking? Come in, sit down. Or shall we help you unpack the car; get that out of the way?"

At last. Deirdre stepped back and allowed me to get out of the car.

This was not really a question more like the next directive. So far Gerard had only uttered greetings of welcome. He glanced occasionally at his wife as she spoke but seemed more interested in his highly polished brown shoes.

"Dahling, do give Laura a hand would you. Come along Mother we'll make tea."

The shoes stirred. The ground was dusty and I was afraid that the sight of the polish diminishing was going to be too much for him.

He coughed nervously into the back of his hand, again. "You would like some 'elp?"

Now considering this immaculately dressed Frenchman looked like he might put his back out lifting a cup and saucer.

I said. "Noo, really, I would rather do it myself. Thank you."

I refrained from adding... for offering.

Had a twin interviewed me in Brixton?

I had just unloaded the television with its built in video player and placed them at the bottom of the stairs when Deirdre walked past with a tea tray laden with Lapsang Souchong, you can't mistake that odour, multi coloured cubed sugar and of course no milk. Betty followed dutifully with an ornate gold rimmed plate (I am guessing one of Betty's) piled high with shortbread.

"I have friend in England who keeps me supplied." Betty explains as if she makes a hobby out of drug trafficking.

Unpacking the car suddenly seemed like a crazy idea. I needed a break.
It was three thirty, a little early for gouter (the equivalent of afternoon tea) and snacking between meals in France is still not advised, so I felt honoured to be a part of the rule breaking.

We all placed ourselves in a semi circle on the terrace in the shade. Deirdre reaches for a huge khaki sun hat, the same colour as her crumpled baggy shorts. Her crisp cotton short- sleeved shirt is bright orange. It is a stark contrast to her very pale almost opaque skin. Her face and arms are interspersed with tiny freckles but none on her legs, I notice. Her short dark russet coloured hair is thick and a similar cut to Gerard's only his is longer in the neck. They look a tad disturbingly like brother and sister.

"Can't have too much sun can I Mother? Not with my colouring."

Deirdre seems to imply that Betty must be responsible for this genetic defect.

Betty merely nodded.

"So. 'ere we all are Movver . You will be 'appy wiv Laura."

Gerard said this in such a way that it was impossible to know if it was a statement or a question.

I am never sure about this son-in-law thing, calling their mother-in-law, Mother. It always seems to smack of ...That is it; you are stuck with me now. A bit too desperate to be accepted.

Betty leaned across and tapped me on the knee.

"Excellent choice Gerard. I am sure we will both be very happy together."

Oh the nuances of language. I had a feeling Betty was right. Deirdre was already leaning back in her chair, eyes closed and now suddenly Gerard looked relaxed or was it relieved. To my surprise he leant across the table and placed a cup and saucer in front of each of us. He poured Betty's cup first, then mine, then Deirdre's. He sat back and poured a cup for himself, at the same time indicating the sugar bowl to me. I took two lumps. I was exhausted.

"So 'ow was your trip?" Gerard seemed to be on automatic pilot.

"Long but uneventful; thanks."

It seemed pointless to elaborate. I had spoken to them twice on the telephone during my two days travelling.

Although uneventful was not quite accurate. However, the details of my trip were not something I thought they would appreciate but I was beginning to get the distinct impression that Betty would hoot.

"Cheers," said Betty raising her cup parallel to her nose.

"You say this with tea, maman?"

Poor Gerard. He had had two English women to cope with, now he had three.

But not for long. Gerard and Deirdre were leaving on Wednesday. I was wondering how Betty felt about the swimming pool when she caught my eye, raising her left eyebrow. I wish I could do that.

****

It was seven thirty by the time I had fully unloaded the car and installed it in my room. A room big enough to swing several cats end to end. About thirty metres square. All the walls were painted pale lemon. The floor had terracotta tiles with skirting boards the same colour. Very practical.

There was a brand new double bed. Deirdre had asked what I would like. I said I liked to spread out. A large wooden table, for writing, a comfortable deep buttoned blue armchair, for reading and a large chest of drawers in a dark, highly polished wood. No wardrobe, that I could see but then I realised that the far wall had three panels with pale blue flowers, apparently painted by hand. They were sliding doors. Wardrobe and shelves appeared. Hmm. I could live here, I chuckled to myself.

The wall facing east and the front of the house had three windows, all opening inwards, as they do here and two large French windows opening from a balcony.

I could see Beryl from there. Although, Gerard had pointed out that it was best to leave my car half way up the drive, under the pine trees as the last few yards was full of pot holes. Not good for the suspension. I nearly asked if that was the problem with their car but thought better of it. There was no sign of another car but I hadn't seen the back of the property yet. I knew there was a back garden and that Betty insisted on having the top floor and therefore lots of stairs because it was dual aspect and was always light.

I searched the room for hidden doors. En-suite, the advert had said. Uh-oh. No car, no television. Was this the hat trick? Questions will be asked at supper.

Tuesday 27th June.

Paradise Continued.

"Homesick already?" It was Betty standing behind me. I hadn't heard her come downstairs.

"Oh, gosh no, I was just phoning my friend to tell her how wonderful it all is."

It was hard to tell her age. In fact if anything she looked just radiant.
 Betty's hair was neither grey nor blonde, but somewhere in between. Her face was lined in all the usual places but it still seemed to have a baby soft quality to it. Her long dark lashes devoid of mascara, gave her a girlish look. This life obviously suited her. Betty dragged one of the white painted patio chairs, metal against stone shattering the peace and sat alongside me. I suddenly thought... did she know Doris...maybe they were related? It was that recycled teenager twinkle in the eyes that did it.
Betty was dressed in a white cotton kimono with two strategically placed appliquéd pink fuchsias.
"Think you'll stay then?"

"Are you kidding? When do Deirdre and Gerard go?"

Betty laughed. "Want to get the cover off the pool, by any chance?"

I nodded as I grabbed my oversized blue and yellow cup off the table. "Can't wait. Breakfast?"

"Did they tell you about the van?"

"Oh yes, at the end of the drive. I haven't heard it yet."

"Don't worry he comes here last."

On cue a klaxon horn sounded three times. Betty waved a fifty franc note at me.

"Just get pain au chocolat or pain aux raisins; we'll get bread when we go out. I'll explain later."

I put my cup back on the table and slipped into my sandals.

****

"Is it usually this warm, this early?" I looked at Betty as she nibbled at the hard chocolate sticking out of her pain au chocolat.

"You mean in the day or in the year?"

"Um, both I suppose."

"Yes and yes." Betty was swirling the rich buttery dough in the froth of her coffee. "And you still want to stay even though I've told you the truth?" She kicked off her flat silk slippers and put her feet up on the seat next to me.

I was wearing my old faithful denim shorts, which were in danger of splitting at the seams, especially if the food and pace of life were to continue.

"Oh sure. I'm all for people taking control of their lives. I reckon I might learn a lot from you."

I tapped her feet with my left hand. Her tanned skin was amazingly soft *for her age*, I thought.

I'd already promised never to use the expression out loud but I couldn't help thinking it.

"So tell me, how was your journey, anything interesting happen?"

Betty had taken an emery board from the mysterious depths of her kimono and was filing the nail on her left little finger.

I moved my chair slightly so as to direct the sun out of my eyes and onto my shoulders.

"Interesting?" I echoed.

"Yes. When you arrived yesterday, every now and then you'd drift off. I'm betting it was a recent experience."

"Does Deirdre know you're psychic?"

"Oh *no* dear. That would be a lot less fun!"

I couldn't decide how much to tell her. I mean she seemed so uninhibited. But would she think I was going to be unreliable; go off with first Romeo to appear, leaving her uncared for?

"Come on. Or I shall tell Deirdre to send you back"

For a moment I thought she was serious. Then she threw her head back and laughed like a drain.

"Okay. I'll do you a deal," she leant forward, screwing up her eyes in mock menace, "I'll tell you about Jean-Louis, if you tell me what was making you smile yesterday...deal?"

She held out her hand; now perfectly manicured.

"Who's Jean-Louis?" I asked.

"Uh oh. No you don't. You first and don't spare the details."

"Well, the first thing he said was, 'you're English!' in the kind of voice previously used by some scientists discovering DNA. And I thought, this is going to be fun."

Betty raised her right hand, school girl style. "Erm, Laura, who's he and where did you meet him?"

"Ah sorry Betty. It was after Calais at the first service station on the A26 just before Arras, junction…"

"Good grief, you go from one extreme to the other. Motorway rest stop would do."

"True. Anyway…"

I glanced at Betty who was giggling already and I had not told her anything funny yet. The perfect audience. She rotated her right hand in an effort to get me to continue.

"Anyway, to describe him as eager would do him an injustice. He was pure adrenalin on legs. He'd parked his black VW alongside my yellow and black Renault 5 and…"

I stopped as Betty was waving at my car parked underneath one of the pine trees. I had told her my car was called Beryl and she was now mouthing 'Will she ever get to the good bits Beryl?'

"I was sat in the car park and I sensed him before I saw him, so I opened my door; he opened his. I hesitated; he shut his. Wow, not bad! I looked at my watch, only two hours since my tyres had touched French tarmac. Then we got out at the same time and he asked if I was going to get a drink or something to eat. I said both, so he asked if he could buy me a cup of coffee. You know what, Betty, if only I had a fiver for every time I'd heard that one."

Betty nodded, and hitched her kimono up above her knees. I couldn't help but notice her excellent pins, no varicose veins, just the odd thread veins round the knees. Her toe nails were adorned with the obligatory old ladies peach nail polish; nothing flashy or vulgar. I was still hesitating over just how much to tell Betty but her eyes wide open with anticipation seemed to give me the answer. So I went on.

"We walked over the covered bridge that connects the south bound carriageway to the rest stops. His heavy boots clattered on the metal walkway. A coach load of children were gaining on us, their voices echoing in the enclosed space. He seemed to know the way so I let him lead and we chatted in a very long queue in Franglais. I explained that I was driving down to Marseille to start a new job looking after an elderly lady."

Betty looked around, eyebrows raised as if expecting someone to appear.

I kept a straight face and gave an innocent shrug, the first of many.

"He looked puzzled so I suggested...like a nanny. He looked delighted and said that he was only a little boy who needed looking after! Somehow I doubted this; he looked like one of those slender bods with a nicely disproportionate..." I hesitated.

"Go on." said Betty.

"Um... erection."

I side glanced Betty's smile.

"Ah what the heck, I thought, we were enjoying ourselves. I felt as though a fresh new face had appeared. Last night's tired face now left in the car. My hormones were reaching simmering point. And to top it all, my new friend not only had an interesting name he had an equally interesting job, as well. He said it was something to do with jewellery, but not like that, he was pointing at the ring on my right hand. No, much more interesting...body piercing! So of course I immediately apologised for only having my ears pierced. Very English. Then I looked him up and down, we were in the restaurant queue by this time..." I glanced at Betty who had her eyes closed but she nodded so I went on.

"Foolishly, I wondered out loud, why he didn't advertise his wares. At which point he started to pull out his shirt and then undo his belt, oh my god, I thought, not here in the middle of the restaurant, surely..."

Betty peered over the top of her sunglasses.

"No, not there," I said in answer to Betty's silent question. "He had a ring through his belly button. I looked around; no-one else seemed bothered, amused yes but bothered no."

"So what was his name?" Betty was all ears.

"Well, I mean why, I wanted to ask, had his parents seen fit to name their son after a car part or better still an aging female rock star. So there he was Axel, full of anticipation and promise, balancing a tray each, we headed outside.
We sat at one of those wooden tables with the bench seats built in. You know the sort where you have to clamber over and try not to lose your balance. It was warm and very windy. We shrieked at each other's pronunciations. He said he had been working in Folkestone, but managed to say it over four syllables, took me ages to work it out.
 He picked at his salad. I wolfed down my chicken and ratatouille. It was only eleven but I was hungry. I asked if his salad was okay, so he started eating heartily, as if to please me. So I thought, perhaps he was just a little boy after all."

"Ah, that's it!" Betty sat up, her eyes wide with excitement.

"That's what?" I wondered.

"That expression, the one you had yesterday."

"Oh yes," I agreed sheepishly.

"Well, go on."

"I put the plastic cover back over my plate. It was one of those with a hole in the middle. I stuffed my paper serviette into the hole, leaving half pointing upwards. He immediately leant forward and pretended to light it....poof....a Molotov cocktail. Only we didn't throw it...Aha, he exclaimed, a terrorist. You guessed, I agreed. A terrorist of... he pondered for a moment, then clutching his chest, preening with genius he said... a terrorist of the heart.
Honestly, I don't know if it was the warmth, the food or his accent but his words were having a powerful effect. And, yes I was tempted but I had a job to get to by tomorrow night I reminded him, and I still had five hundred miles to go. So I decided I had been fed, watered and charmed so I was ready to continue my journey. He was totally perplexed. 'You're leaving?' he says.
I told him I was. We walked back to our cars. While we were eating we had been discussing star signs, so I reached in to my car for a magazine (it was in French) so he could see the word for Aries. His had been easy. Libra the scales, but do you think I could get him to understand Aries the ram. I had tried what I thought was the French for lamb or sheep and added male, but to no avail. I could of course have just sat there in the restaurant and gone, baa! But we were sat next to four very English ladies (and I do mean English) who thought our conduct most unbecoming as it was. Need I say more?"

"Not like me then?" Betty asked pretending to look hurt.

I rolled my eyes, already knowing that Betty and I were already on the same wavelength. I continued. "Axel looked at the model on the back cover of the magazine and said it was me. The night before, maybe but talk about charm, was he born with it I wondered? I was pretty sure it wasn't *Maybelline*."

"Pardon?" said Betty.

I waved my hand dismissively.

"Oh nothing, sorry, too much television."

"So the moment had come. Was it goodbye or just au revoir? Should I give him my phone number or just go. Should we shake hands or the customary peck on each cheek? You know it's at moments like these that I'm sure the Martians must be watching us, clutching their sides and saying. Look, look, the earthlings are still having problems communicating."

"How true. Refill?"

Betty was moving her chair back and reaching for my cup.

"Um, aren't I supposed to be doing that?"

"Nah, you can do it all when Deirdre's around, otherwise we'll take it in turns. Don't forget where you got to."

She disappeared through the huge open plan living room, gliding across the polished tiles in her satin flip flops and into the kitchen.

"Have you got some sun screen on?" she shouted back at me.

"No, that's true. I'll do it now."

I went upstairs two at a time. I peered into the mirror. I couldn't believe my luck. I half expected to see another face mocking me. *And you thought this was real*? I scooped up my blonde bob out of the way using my sunglasses; they always seemed more comfortable somehow, on top of my head, before smoothing a large blob of factor fifteen around tired eyes. It had been difficult to sleep last night.

The double bed was comfortable, the smell of a brand new cotton duvet cover and sheets, reassuring but I was distracted by the sounds of the trees rustling outside my balcony, the birds and their dawn chorus, and the sight of a red squirrel hopping from branch to branch at five a.m. I needed sleep but I wanted to get out there and explore my new life.

I poured some cool water from a matching jug into an old fashioned white porcelain bowl, adorned with blue cornflowers and splashed my face.

Sorry it's not en-suite. Deirdre had apologised, last night, before I had chance to ask. We are having a basin put in for you next week.

But it hardly mattered, as tomorrow they were off to Italy, I would have the bathroom to myself. And Betty had her own bathroom upstairs, en-suite. In my pad, as she called it.

****

"So, where were we?"

A fresh pot of coffee sat in the middle of the table. Alongside was a plate with two nectarines cut into quarters. I could get used to this.

"Oh yes, Axel informs me that he has family in Marseille. He's going to visit them in August, so maybe I'll see him then. He hands me a catalogue. It's called The Wildcat Collection. Sophisticated body adornment products. He writes his mobile phone number on the back. The book's in English, which is just as well because there are some words I've never heard of, places to be pierced; some of them make my eyes water, just thinking about them but they fascinate me all the same. I complained enough when I had my ears pierced so don't think my labia are going to be next!"

Betty spluttered as she half swallowed her coffee.

"Oh God, I'm sorry, are you okay? But you said leave nothing out."

"It's okay, it's okay, carry on. I haven't had this much fun since I left my friend Audrey back in England. Go on."

"You're sure?"

She didn't look shocked exactly, more bemused, so I continued.

"Anyway, I was intrigued by the idea that a rep's job might include checking out various body parts for suitability. I had visions of him saying...'Now madam, are yoo sure yoo vant a bell on your clitoris?'

I said, trying to imitate a French male accent and failing.

Betty rocked on her chair so hard I was afraid that she was going to tip up.

She waved for me to go on.

"So, he was stood facing me, reading my thoughts, who knows, but he was smiling anyway. So I gave him my new phone number and said, maybe see you in August then? I held out my hand, he took it. I started to shake it, he tutted, he put my hand to his mouth and then said, 'No...no...Come here.'

He pulled me firmly to him, watching my reaction the whole time. I could have said no.

So there we were in the middle of this auto route car park, leaning against my car...kissing. After a few seconds he stopped and complained that kissing with your mouth closed was not on! I decided to call it a day. I was not ready for anymore. After a shower and a change of clothes, perhaps, but this was neither the time nor the place."

Betty's lower lip protruded in disappointment.

"Okay so sometimes I'm boring."

"He looked forlorn, but didn't press the issue. He was heading back north. I was continuing south. It wasn't until sometime later that I wondered how we met; both on the same side of the motorway. I drove off with a smile on my face. Oh to be in France now that June is here. So as I drove along, the overhead signs said things like 'conduire ou dormir'...drive or sleep. Good advice, I always think."

Betty nodded, closing her eyes against the sun.

I sighed and surveyed my surroundings.

A light breeze was wafting along the drive, picking up the essence of pine needles along the way. I wanted to capture this moment. Put it in a bottle. Capture it for all time. So back in England some soulless grey day, I could pop the cork and let a little reminder of perfection wash over me. I didn't realise I had stopped talking until Betty said. "That's not the end is it?"

"Oh, no...And then the temperature comes up...19 degrees...a few kilometres more and it's 22...Aah...24 and so on. It's always been one of my favourite things, to drive south, watch the day unfold and the temperature rise. And this time I was alone. The freedom of the open road..."

Betty let out an 'Mmm' in agreement.

ALL EXPENSES PAID

"The sunroof open for the first time this year, the music loud, I was cruising at 120k (the speed limit) I'm content. Do you drive Betty?"

She opened one eye. "Yes," she said then added, "but not recently," and winked before closing her eyes again. "Go on!"

"So why is the car behind me flashing its headlights, I wondered. Yep, you guessed it. Axel. He overtakes and indicates the next rest stop ahead. He drives in. I drive past. It's one of those lovely wooded areas with tables and bench seats, like the ones back at the restaurant, loos and telephones and not much else. I'm tempted, but not enough. I drive on. Within a few minutes he's there, behind me again, oh dear, how long will he keep this up? He drives alongside me. I've dropped back to 110k now, so he is blocking the middle lane. No-one seems to mind, no lights flashing, horns blaring. It's pretty obvious what is going on. You have to hand it to the French they have their priorities right."

"Weren't you worried?" Betty had moved onto the recliner underneath one of the pine trees.

"No, I can't say I was. Perhaps I should have been. Anyway, I glance across at him. He's smiling, waving and pointing to the next exit. I shake my head. I look across again and there held in his hand, between finger and thumb, like a trophy, up pops a condom!

He probably couldn't tell if I was saying no, I was laughing so much. So, off he shoots, (pardon the pun) taking the next exit into the woods. "

"Really?" says Betty in between chewing the last nectarine segment. She's had five pieces, but who's counting?

"Really." I confirmed.

"And what did you do?" Betty had sat upright again so she can see the expression my face. She didn't miss a trick.

"I drove on, but it made my day. His way of saying Fol..kes...ton...e. Lighting my terrorist lunch and now waving a condom, in case I was unsure, I mean, don't you just love it! Why waste time. The world could end tomorrow and what better way to a woman's heart than to wave a condom."

"And they say romance is dead," Betty chortled.

I confessed I hadn't really unpacked, so I went up to my room. Betty promised she wanted nothing from me today. I was to unpack and make myself at home. We'd had a salad lunch with freshly grated carrot, celeriac, plump raisins, teeny weeny grey prawns, endives and shaved parmesan, followed by more fresh fruit and some red wine. It's good for me, thank God, she'd said.
 Julia had phoned to say she was doing a double shift so couldn't talk to me tonight. I told her I'd write her a letter. Or at least finish the one I had started. I grabbed my dictaphone and some writing paper. I wound back to the beginning and started to write. I had just got to the bit where I was telling her about my first stop on the auto-route when I heard a car coming up the gravel driveway. Must be Deirdre and Gerard or Dolce and Gabbana, as Betty insisted on calling them behind their backs. Another of her little secrets. I continued the letter with... *I was telling Betty all about it this morning. You can tell her anything. Imagine Doris with a tan, more money but less jewellery.*
And then I remembered. Jean-Louis, she hadn't told me about Jean-Louis! I leapt up from the seat on my balcony, just in time to see Betty rearranging herself on the terrace. She'd had her legs up on the table reading a Jackie Collins novel.

ALL EXPENSES PAID

Jackie Collins was deftly slid into the knitting bag at the side of her chair and out came half the back of a bed jacket in pale pink. Betty glanced up. She knew I was watching her. Jean-Louis was going to have to wait until tomorrow, damn. I ended Julia's letter with a quick, *tell you the rest when we speak*. I was not sure how long the post would take and I knew I would have to tell her all about Axel. I folded the letter and stuffed it an envelope. Time to go and make polite conversation with my new employers.

Wednesday 28th June

An Expected Visitor.

"Oh and there is just one other thing."

Gerard put down the two cases on the patio, obviously hoping that the taxi driver would get out of his car and put them in the boot whilst Deirdre went off into presumably yet another tale of the bleeding obvious.

"I forgot to mention, every summer, well the four that I've been here, I have tried to fit in with everyone of course, it's the only way isn't it?"

I had already developed the essential nod that Betty and Gerard used in the hope that she would get to the point sometime soon.

"So as I say, every summer they hold a music festival here in the village, well, not just in the village, in Martigues as well but everyone acts as hosts to the visiting musicians, oh and dancers too."

She paused for breath. Gerard is poised just inside the sliding glass doors, eyeing the taxi. The driver has not moved, his left arm dangles from the driver's window and he periodically taps ash from his roll up onto the ground.

"They come from all over the world."

She looks at me expectantly. I decide amazement would be appropriate. She acknowledged my reaction and continued. "So this year it just happens to coincide with our trip. It will be wonderful for you. I'm really going to miss it all. It's such fun!"

A short sharp beep from the taxi made us all jump.

Gerard hurried forth from the patio towards the cases.

"Cheri, we will miss our flight."

Deirdre gasps as if she has only just been told she is going on holiday and lurches towards the two cases, picks them both up with ease and levers the boot open with one of them. Gerard opens the rear passenger door for her.

Deirdre swiftly produces yet another neatly typed sheet of information from her enormous brown crocodile handbag. It seemed such an odd choice for a vegetarian.

I glanced at the type written information.

Ten days visit. Lithuanian dance troupe. 1 person to stay. Bed and bed breakfast only. Plus lift into village morning and back in the evening.

There followed a list of names and phone numbers. A complete guide to the ten days events with a little # by the side of the ones she felt sure I would like.

I had the feeling it was deemed imperative that I go. Maybe she would ask questions when she came back. Agh!

In her immaculate handwriting she had added at the bottom. **You will hardly know he is here**. Betty was now standing alongside me on the edge of the patio. The four magnificent pine trees providing shade from the midday sun. We hardly dared look at each other as Gerard and Deirdre finally settled into the back of the taxi. Deirdre started to wind down the window. The taxi driver hit the accelerator so hard that Gerard was flung back in his seat. Deirdre blew us both a kiss and shouted "Have fun!"

We knew she didn't mean a word of it. So we took great delight in silently mouthing, 'We will,' at the cloud of dust.

I looked again at the sheet of paper for the arrival date and time. Great. Five pm today.

****

"So come on Betty, your turn."

"OK, but I think I need a siesta first."

"Oh no you don't, I told you all about Axel yesterday."

"Yes and that's the trouble I can't really compete with that."

"Don't be silly Betty I just want to know about you and Jean-Louis."

We drag the chairs underneath the shade of the pine trees.

"So come on; how did you meet?"

"Well, let me see, I'd been here a while and Deirdre was worried that I was going to get homesick, so she decided that I needed to meet some expats."

"So where did she take you?"

Betty rolls her eyes and sighs. "A bridge club in Martigues called Bridge for Blighties."

"I don't really see you as a bridge player Betty."

"Oh really?"

"Really. Did you enjoy it?"

"Well I..."

"Did you go in Betty?"

"Deirdre plays poker you know and she thought a card game would be good for my brain."

"You don't like cards do you?"

Betty shakes her head with a smirk.

"Me neither."

"So what did you do?"

"I waited until D was out of sight and hot footed it across the road to the cafe. It's my regular now. Takes them all afternoon to play a rubber." Betty eyes me with a mischievous look.

"Oh no, you don't get me there. I know a rubber is something to do with bridge. You spent, what, four hours in a cafe? Anyway hang on, you still haven't told me about Jean-Louis."

"Ah well you see, whilst I was being deposited to play bridge with the boring retired set, Jean-Louis was investigating the line dancing club next door. His brother was a member and thought he might like it. He had peered around the door and realised the female to male ratio was nine to one. He said he would feel like a blue bottle trapped in a jar."

"Okay, so the bridge club and the line dancing took place at the same time. The room must have been well soundproofed ...?"

Betty shrugged. "You're not going to become all practical on me are you Laura?"

"Oh, no, just a thought. So you bumped into each other in the entrance and it was love at first sight?"

"No, but almost. As I said I went to the cafe opposite and ordered a pot of tea and a crêpe with Nutella. Which of course I'm not allowed since my stroke."

"Huh. A little bit of what you fancy does you good."

"You can stay." Betty gives me her best grin.

"And now you're going to tell me that Jean-Louis had a part-time job as a waiter in the cafe?" Betty grins as she enjoys her chance to be the storyteller.

"No but the waiter returns and says: Thé et crêpes?"

"I raised my hand at exactly the same moment as the man at the table next to me. The waiter of course served me first. Jean-Louis giving an exaggerated half bow. The waiter returned with a duplicate order for Jean-Louis. He poured himself a cup of tea, raising his cup in my direction with a perfectly pronounced. Your good health."

"Ah, so he speaks English?"

"Like a native. And even better, he has the same sense of humour."

"And Deirdre thinks?"

"Yep, I spend four hours per week playing bridge. And meeting nice cultured English people."

"You're very different aren't you; you and your daughter."

"Very. She's never forgiven me for naming her after a character in Coronation Street."

"Ah yes, she erm..."

"Go on..? She told you that?"

"No not exactly just that she wasn't keen on her name and to call her just D."

"Do you know I used to feel so guilty that if she telephoned me when I was watching Coronation Street I used to turn down the sound. Even though my daughter was born before Deirdre appeared in Corrie. Her disapproval can be quite withering but she's not all bad and certainly she's happy with Gerard."

"No children?"

Betty looked startled and I realised I had spoken out of turn.

"Sorry Betty, it just came out."

"Don't worry but at least you didn't ask them. Time's running out now of course with Deirdre being forty seven this year. They've had all the tests, both of them, nothing seems to be wrong. This is why I'm so glad they've gone on this trip."

Betty glances away for a moment. She suddenly looks like an eighty two year old lady.

One with regrets. But in an instant she is back.

"Remind me to show you something in the study when we go in."

I nod. "Anyway, back to Jean-Louis and have Deirdre or Gerard met him yet?"

"Oh no dear, that's half the fun for both of us. They think I'm playing bridge and Jean–Louis' brother thinks he's line dancing. Got to get your fun where you can."

"And where is that exactly?"

"Laura, have you ever heard of the word discreet or tactful?"

I had turned down my mouth and raised my eyes to the sky to ponder.

"Very funny Laura. Shall we pop down to the beach cafe for lunch?"

"Good idea but when am I going to meet Jean-Louis?"

"He'll be around tomorrow to take the cover off the pool for us and even more importantly how to put it back on. There is a knack."

****

The plat du jour was fresh salmon, basmati and wild rice with fennel. Delicious. Betty had a carafe of rosé. I took one sip and decided to stick to Vittel. After ice cream and coffee, whilst dangling our toes in the Med, I dropped Betty back at the ranch before heading off to Martigues to collect our new arrival. The drive would take about twenty minutes on the auto-route, Deirdre had assured me but I preferred to take the scenic route. I'd had enough of motorways for a while. Thirty five minutes later I arrived in the Provencal town that would become my second home over the next six months.

ALL EXPENSES PAID

Wednesday 28thth June. 5pm.

A Dancer from Lithuania.

A lesson in Melancholy.

As the coach pulled into the village square I made a pact. Please god let him be, was going to say tall dark and handsome but no, god is probably sick of those requests so I just settled for fun. Do Lithuanians 'do' fun? I am not being racist here, I just mean humour. There is such a division between cultures. Being a Midlander, some might say, Brummie, I can do my fair share of sarcasm. This does not go down well with the French and I must admit I have found it much more irritating since I moved away- i.e. south of Watford. But I digress.

Pay attention Laura, the coach doors are opening. Be a good idea to hold up the sign with our new guest's name on it. Deirdre of course had already made the sign out of cardboard and used jolly coloured felt tip pens. His name is surrounded by pictures of sunshine and smiley faces. Betty confirmed that Deirdre had been an avid Blue Peter watcher in her girlhood. In the end, Betty told me, she had to buy a dishwasher or Deirdre would stand over her waiting for the next empty washing up bottle...

With a whoosh and a clang the coach doors are firmly open and I momentarily let the name card drop to my side. Why not let everyone get off and see who is left? Genius. Then if he looks like he might smell, snore loudly or sing before 7 am, I could just wander off. However if he has washing up hands (Betty's idea, as the nice man in the village can't fix the dishwasher until Friday) or understands the custom of bringing morning tea to two ladies in bed, I can produce the sign with an apologetic flourish. Manipulative...moi?

I am still holding the name card at a hundred and eighty degrees, close to my thigh when (oh, so there is a God) an amused six foot Adonis tilts his head to read the Lithuanian name inscribed on the card. They have to be the tightest blue jeans I have ever seen, and in this heat. It is thirty two degrees this afternoon and no discernable breeze. So sticky, just about sums up the situation. Adonis is wearing the regulation white tee shirt with the name of his dance troupe emblazoned across it. I can't pronounce that name either. Deirdre assured me that he spoke some English. But then Deirdre had been married to a Frenchman too long to remember that if you don't know the answer to something you should not make it up in the guise of being helpful.

"Oh hi." I raise my eyes all the way up to meet his. He simply nods. His thick brown locks fall across his forehead and I resist the temptation to reach up and...

"Vous parlez Angalis?"

"Oui." I said.

Now, my new charge looks really confused because it was him asking me if I spoke English and I replied in French. Duh. Obviously my 'Oh hi' was not English enough. So we began again.

"Do you have luggage?" I asked pointing to the coach driver unloading bags from the hold.

Adonis' real name begins with an E but with no other vowels; I decided to call him Ed. I will tell him later, just so he knows.

As he hauls his rucksack onto the back seat of my R5, I open the passenger door for him. He of course looks confused until he realises it is a right hand drive.

I have begged Betty to hang on in the house until I get back with our new charge. Betty had nodded, sympathising with the fact that I had only just arrived and Deirdre had 'thrown me in the deep end'. If only. It was now thirty four degrees and a mistral was expected anytime soon. A breeze would be nice, but no need for the three day extravaganza that whips everything up into a frenzy leaving cars covered with sand from the Sahara. Jean-Louis will get the cover off the pool for us when he comes this evening and show us how to put in back on in an emergency.

You mean if D and G come home early? I had asked Betty. She nodded.

Poor old (probably twenty years younger than me) Ed looked shattered. Should we try and make conversation? Will he think me rude if we don't? How much English does he speak?

"It's just a ten minute drive to the house."

I smile at him, raising both hands at the same time. Universal speak to indicate ten minutes? He nods as his eyelids flutter. Poor lamb. I start the engine and Ed leans towards the radio giving me a querying look. "Sure." I keep it simple. He looks puzzled. Not simple enough. Think universal words and signs. Think; Christmas after Christmas of charades.

"Yes, ok."

Ah. Better. He turns on the radio. It is tuned to NRJ. Robbie Williams springs to life...

Ed rests his head against the headrest. At least he can reach it. I am coming back as a tall man in my next life. The world seems to fit them better.

It is five o'clock by the time we get back to the house and Ed is jolted awake as I pull up too abruptly, at the edge of the patio. No Gerard here to grizzle about disturbing the gravel. If Ed had been surprised to meet me, how was he going cope with wonder-woman?

I watched as Ed's eyes opened to their maximum and locked into a glazed stare. I suddenly wondered what the French word was for stroke as he looked in serious danger of having one. Betty surely must have heard us but I did not like to pip my horn. Ed blinked. Phew. His breathing had resumed and I gave him my most reassuring sideways grin. The grin that said, ok this *is* the asylum but I know where the back door and escape route are.

I turned off the radio and realised that Spandau Ballet were not after all in the living room but reverberating from the ghetto blaster that Betty normally kept in her room. Ed titled his head until it touched his left shoulder. Betty blinked furiously. I was so glad she did not try and wave. Ed and I watched, mesmerized as Betty brought her legs back down to the ground and elegantly unfurled from her head stand. Great for the circulation, she had assured me when I had been greeted by the upside down Betty yesterday evening, in her room. 'Can't have too much circulation. Stroke prevention. Plus, she insisted, it helps defy that permanent advisory; gravity.'

Of course as a dancer Ed was no stranger to limbering up in a yogic fashion but I think what really took his breath away was the fact that Betty had unleashed a whole new wardrobe for the occasion. Her puce leggings glimmered in the late afternoon sun and her white tee shirt read: ***Sisters are doing it for themselves***. Although from what Betty had already told me about Jean-Louis, was neither true nor necessary. I switched off the engine and Betty waved.

Ed's eyes did a tour of their sockets. Before I could say anything Betty was opening his door and extending a hand. "Welcome, bienvenue...what's that in Lithuanian Laura?"

I shrugged. "Don't worry; I think Ed gets the message."

Ed allowed himself to be hauled out of the car by Betty before he found his voice. He introduced himself with a half bow. Betty curtseyed. Good grief.

Whatever next? I showed Ed to his room. Betty went into the kitchen to prepare tea. Giving Ed one more quick appraisal, I would guess he was either not a cake eater or had a metabolism to kill for.

He was going to be using the tiny single bedroom, usually used for storage. He glanced at the bed. Thoughts of Gulliver's travels came to mind. Maybe I should offer him D and G's room. I will see what Betty thinks. I led him into the bathroom and explained how to switch the taps from bath to shower. He gave me a look I shall never forget as he said. "I'm foreign, not stupid."

Yikes. I explained that Betty was making tea and he should come and join us when he was ready. Two hours later Betty and I looked at each other. What to do? I went up and tapped on his closed door. Ed opened the door a smidgen. He had an earplug in his left ear and out of the right side was dangling a wire. I held up a takeaway pizza menu. He nodded, said okay and shut the door. He looked so forlorn. And for once I did not have a plan.

Betty had showered and joined me on the terrace wearing a calf length lemon seersucker dress. "You can't see the creases." She nodded in my direction with a grin. Jean-Louis was coming to pick her up at eight o'clock. I had ordered pizza for me and chatterbox. Betty thought I was being too hard on him. He could be suffering from any number of emotions. Give him a chance. As always, a word from the wise, aka Betty.

I soon discovered that the French love takeaway pizzas as much as their Italian neighbours. So the sound of yet another approaching motorbike, changing gear as it reached the end of the drive was no surprise. Only this bike did not have a square red box on the back. A serviceable scooter it was not. More like a giant black insect. A turbo charged one at that. It was driven, or rather propelled by a lithe gentleman clad in jeans and a black leather jacket. A black crash helmet with an orange flash across the front completed the outfit. A matching crash helmet dangled from the left handlebar.

Helen Ducal

Matters of health and safety?

Uh-oh. Betty had started to tell me about Jean-Louis last night and the fact that he was taking her out tonight but mode of transport seemed to have been omitted. Now what was I supposed to do? Betty was obviously compos mentis ...more than many people half her age but I was being paid to look after her. Did this come under the heading of; I never interfere except in matters of health and safety? Yes, definitely. But how the heck could I prevent it?

Luckily for Betty the aforementioned pizza delivery bike appeared at exactly the same moment as Ed walked onto the terrace, bleary eyed and crumpled. Ed looked in disbelief as Jean-Louis hopped off his pulsating beast, ran over to Betty, scooped her up, round her waist with one arm, and plonked her astride the pillion of his bike in one very deft move. The pizza guy turned out to be a girl who had stopped alongside Jean-Louis' beast, a Kawasaki 1200, and let out a 'Genial,' as Betty quickly placed the spare helmet on her head. The pizza girl was staring at Ed who had apparently not fully recovered from waking up, as his shorts had a discernible tilt to starboard. His very long brown legs encased in flip flops and bed hair completed his look.

"Don't wait up!" Betty shrieked.

I followed the pizza girl's gaze and Ed started to tremble with embarrassment.

This was not going well.

I paid the pizza girl and went into the kitchen to get plates and cutlery. By the time I got back onto the terrace Ed had devoured half of the pizza. He handed me the open box and mumbled goodnight. I was about to ask about breakfast

ALL EXPENSES PAID

and whether he needed a lift and what time in the morning but he was already at the top of the stairs. Ah well. I supposed I would hear him moving about and it was not as though I was expected to produce full English. In the meantime I could worry about what time little Miss- head -stand would rock up. So far, more had happened in three days here, than in three weeks with my first job. I put the clean plates and cutlery back in the kitchen and went to my room. The beauty of such warm weather meant I could be dressed in a jiffy but I got my clean jeans and turquoise tee shirt out ready for the morning.

I was just drifting off to sleep when I heard the putter of a motorbike engine coming to a halt. Jean-Louis had obviously parked at the end of the driveway to avoid the sound of scattering gravel permeating the house. I wondered if Ed was asleep yet. Maybe he was just out of his comfort zone. Not everyone is as chatty as you and I, Betty had chastised me. "He'll come round. He's probably nervous about the dance festival and meeting so many new people."

With the reassuring sound of Betty's kitten heels click clacking on the stone stairs at the back of the house, I turned out my light. I had set the alarm for seven, giving me chance to use the bathroom and start breakfast before Ed appeared, or so I assumed.

Thursday 29th June.

Mis-communication.

As lovely as the pale lemon curtains in my bedroom were, they let in way too much light. So much for setting the alarm clock for seven, I had been awake for ages. I looked at the clock. Seven fifteen. Ah well. Another beautiful morning; better get up. I would have a shower later when I had got rid of, (still not giving Ed the benefit of the doubt) our guest. Who would have thought that a twenty something Adonis would be less fun than an eighty two year old woman...So far.

I couldn't be bothered to dress, so pulled on my pink shorts. This would allow my baggy white tee shirt (the one with the shark on it, opening a bottle of lager with its teeth) to become decent. I may need to reach up for something in the kitchen.

I flip flopped down to the kitchen expecting to find everything as I had left it the night before. The dishwasher was still full of clean stuff, thankfully it had stopped working after the final rinse but I decided I would empty it in the morning.

The sight of Ed, wearing tight black swimming trunks and holding a pot of yoghurt in his hand was not what I had been expecting.

"Good morning." He said and almost smiled. He still looked tired but not quite so much like the rabbit caught in the headlights. I glanced down at his damp trunks and quickly realised that Jean-Louis must have taken the cover off the pool as promised. Thank goodness.

He glanced at the kitchen clock and said "Eight o' clock. We go."

I nodded as I grabbed the box of muesli from the wall cupboard above the kettle. No problem, thanks to the pink shorts. I opened the dishwasher door to retrieve a clean bowl only to find it empty. This time Ed smiled as he reached across me and opened the next wall cupboard door and handed me a large white cereal bowl and then got milk from the fridge. I thanked him and retreated to the living room. I fancied a comfy chair. I flicked on the radio which I kept on low volume. Did not want to disturb sleeping beauty.

I need not have worried.

"Morning all." It was Betty of course, appearing from the side of the house, carrying a large peach bath towel and yoga mat. She was wearing a purple and pink zigzag patterned swimsuit with matching sarong.

"Oh, morning Betty. Sleep well?"

"I most certainly did. Camomile tea. Works every time. You taking Nureyev soon?"

"Yep, I shall drop him off then come back here. What are your plans for today?"

"Ooh, a bit of this and a bit of that."

It was like asking a recalcitrant teenager.

"Will any of it require my taxi services?" I really hoped not, I was still in somewhat of a daze...

"Nope, don't worry. *You* look like the octogenarian today. Have a lazy day and we'll go out tomorrow. OK?"

"Yes, Betty, you're right, I am still a bit tired."

Before I could say anything else, Ed came bounding down the stairs, two at a time. Sports bag in hand, he smiled at me. "We go?"

We went. I dropped him by the church alongside the harbour. He showed the piece of paper given to him by their dance group leader and this was definitely it, but there were no signs of other athletic limbs. Maybe it was a French eight thirty not an English eight thirty. Meeting the French for coffee often entails patience as twenty minutes either way is considered...c'est normal! I was tempted to stop for a coffee but decided to get back. It was agreed I would pick him up at eight thirty.

When I got back, Betty was dressed in a flowing pale blue kaftan. A matching chiffon scarf did nothing to hide the spongy pink rollers underneath. Her Jackie Collins' novel open and face down, was resting on her knees. Her eyes were closed but her smile told me she was awake. I left her in peace.

****

I drove back into the village to pick Ed up at eight thirty as we had arranged. He looked exhilarated. His hollowed out cheeks had a rosy glow. Does energy create energy I wondered? The show had gone extremely well or at least I think that's what he said.

Back at the ranch, we were standing in the kitchen and I was getting ice for the vodka. He had to like vodka surely; when he brandishes a small red shiny box from an equally shiny, petit carrier bag.

"It is present. Open it." He said placing it in my hand.

Well blow me down, if it wasn't three condoms. I almost expected Axel to appear out of the carrier bag. A touch of déjà vu. And all the time I thought he was playing hard to get. Now because I had been thrown into to the opposite direction for the last twenty four hours I was speechless for a moment before saying. "Only three?"

He laughed and put them away again. I suppose if I am honest, he did show them to me as if they were unusual party gift, and nothing more.

But how was I supposed to know? My hormones had come out of hiding and were getting ready for the fray. So off I went upstairs, it was late and I had already showered, so I just had to wait for him to do the same. I stepped into something more comfortable i.e. as little as possible but still enough to get your teeth into. He dutifully went into the bathroom. Everything it seemed about his life was orderly. He would take twenty minute doing his ablutions, no doubt cleaning his teeth at exactly the same juncture. All this, he told me later was thanks to two years military service, which, he suggested, would do *me* the world of good. I told him to fuck off. Well no actually I didn't.
I said. "Really?"

Then after a moment's contemplation he said, maybe it was necessary for a writer to be undisciplined, to be creative.

Any more comments like that and challenge or no challenge I was going to tell him to get his own breakfast and catch a bus into the village. Any resemblance to Axel, had evaporated.

Ed emerged from the bathroom wearing just a towel but with no signs of activity underneath. I had left my bedroom door open and sat strategically on the sofa with a tumbler of Jack Daniels. I just happened to swizzle my glass (the ice clinked) as he passed my door. He smiled pleasantly, said good night and went into his room and shut the door.

You know that feeling when you think, great, I have just climbed up all these steps to the top of the slide, ready for the ride, and then some prat says, 'Sorry, slide closed. No more rides today.'

Well, there I was, all prepared and ready, with nowhere to go. Even Betty was having more luck than me tonight. I had seen her escaping down the backstairs at nine p.m. A car parked at the edge of the neighbour's driveway looked familiar. Neither of us would mention it. It was more fun this way. So there I was wandering around my room at midnight with an empty glass muttering words of consternation at my plight. Ok, so what I actually said was: Bastard, ungrateful foreign bastard. I have a good mind to get your yoghurt out of the fridge so that it can get warm by breakfast time. His sole topic of conversation this morning had been; lovely cool yoghurt. Even Betty was not back yet. I had just paced to the far end of the room when there was a gentle tap on my door.

Ah. Nice Lithuanian boy come to Laura.

"I do not disturb you?" He probably read it on a hotel doorknob. "Is possible you wake me seven a.m. yes?"

Ah-ha, I thought, he's too tired now so he wants me to wake him earlier in the morning. Of course he is just shy, that's all. Yes, shy, that must be it. Still, difficult: can't remember having to deal with shy before.

"No problem," I said. "Sleep well."

I reached up and gave him a peck on the cheek. Unfortunately it wasn't until two days later that I remembered Julia's advice. So the next morning I was still running on the same track. Perhaps shy means, always having to take the initiative? Perhaps he expected me to follow him back into his room last night? Perhaps I should just pin him to the bloody floor.

Friday 30th June.

The weaker sex?

Six forty five. What a time to have to wake up. Fifteen minutes to shower and apply some hardly there make-up. I shook my head over the balcony to give my hair that morning tousled look. I lay on the bed to zip up my skinny jeans and realised I needed to get my white with red spots boob tube, over my head. So much for the tousled look. It was now more like- rough night was it? I decide a quick splurge of tinted moisturizer and lashings of mascara would help.

He had lent his alarm clock to a friend, he said, which I of course took to mean that he preferred *me* to wake him up.
Good. He was still asleep, but not so good, he was not playing tents. I stood in the open doorway and tried a gentle, "Good morning." I still had not fathomed out how to pronounce his name. He did not stir so I repeated the greeting a little louder. I allowed the two words to develop as meaningfully as possible. "Gooood morning," I repeated.

He raised one hand and then opened his eyes. He smiled. The previous day on the beach had left him glowing. And naked to the waist he was like manna from heaven. Then he pulled the purple duvet up under his chin. Shit, he actually looked scared. He was going to have me crawling up the wall soon.
His body language said goodbye, so I retreated to make breakfast. My patience was running thin. Late nights, early mornings; three in a row and not a glimmer. Still, not one to let a golden opportunity slide by, I applied my hostess with the mostest smile and laid the table out on the terrace.

It was yet another glorious morning, 26° in the shade and only seven fifteen. The crickets were starting their serenade. Funny how some sounds are soothing and others can irritate the hell out of you. For a moment there was no job, no frustrations, just the sun warming the apricots still green for another week or two and then abundance before a battle with the birds and wasps to see who could eat the most. Betty had made apricot jam last year she told me, but she wasn't sure she had the energy this year. No kidding; she hadn't come in until two thirty, tip toeing loudly across the landing above me, still giggling to herself over something Jean- Louis had said, no doubt. It was the first time I have ever been envious of an eighty two year old.

"Boo!"

I practically shot out my chair. Ed was standing behind me, clutching his sides.

"I surprise you?"

"You most certainly did, you little shit."

My huge smile hopefully convinced him that little shit was some kind of endearment. He grabbed a croissant, swallowed a mouthful of coffee, which I had thoughtfully poured for him, and announced. "We go."

Then he raises his right hand but only his index finger in the air. This I had observed, meant that you just remembered something. He ran upstairs. Such energy.

His footsteps were slower coming down. I gauged my journey from the patio to the kitchen and we collided at the bottom of the stairs. We stood for a moment facing each other. It was only a moment but our eyes locked. I was right, the chemistry was there. You know that indescribable tension that builds, waiting to be released .Tonight, tonight, I thought... I would get the blighter. Suddenly, Julia's face popped into my mind. It was wearing a disapproving look. I was behaving like some mad predator. I paused for a moment to consider...The weaker sex? Ha!

I drove him to his meeting spot. I was free all day, free to scheme and plot and imagine. He said he would get a lift back tonight as he would be very late. I said I would appreciate that as I was going out and it would save me hurrying back.

Damn again. There would be no warning of his arrival probably no car lights most people didn't venture up the long drive way to the house, it was full of potholes, not good for the suspension. Even Jean-Louis and he owned a garage wouldn't risk it. So I would just have to be ready with an--Oh, I've just come in myself--look; to be applied at a moment's notice.

It was midnight. The air was wonderfully still, even the crickets were asleep. Despite the mosquitoes I decided to sit on the terrace, candles flickering on the table, glass in hand, Elton John on the CD player. *Sacrifice*. Not the best of songs when you are in the throes of mending a broken heart. Still; no time for maudlin. What's his name could be back at any moment and I was definitely in need of some *Healing Hands*. Elton had moved on. A song for every occasion. That's the thing about our Reg; he has been there, done that and got so many tee-shirts he has sold them for good causes.

I went into the kitchen to check the time. My watch strap had broken and I hadn't replaced it when I realised that I didn't really need it, except when you have to catch a train or a bus. I really wanted to go to bed. Another early start in the morning. I was leaning against the worktop gazing out at the dishevelled garden, when...

"Boo!"

This time I didn't laugh. "You idiot. I could have dropped my glass."

"So sorry," he offered. All my resolve to get my own way; gone in a flash.

"I return for..." He paused, waving his arms about madly in front of him. He went upstairs and returned with his swimming trunks, which he placed on the table. "Ah," he said. The finger rose. He bounded back up the stairs two at a time. I followed at a more leisurely pace. I'd had enough. I was going to bed. I reached my door when he emerged waving a pair of goggles. He started downstairs and then stopped on the second step. He had not seen my serious side before.

"You OK?"

He turned as he said it. I stood at the top of the stairs. This made us the same height. Silently we kissed, tongues gently meeting. Small tingles sent messages but our eyes were sad. It was then that I realized, he too was working, travelling, trying to forget. Obviously he had decided abstinence was the best route.

"Sorry," he said as he ran downstairs and out into the night, to join his mates at a pool party along the road.

Saturday 1st July.

True love.

The next morning Betty's curiosity got the better of her. "So come on; what's he like?"

"Betty," I said despondently. "You know as much as I do."

"What? Oh sorry." She paused as if expecting me to change my expression and admit my latest conquest then she added, as she picked up her coffee" Really?"

"Yes Betty really. You're getting more action than I am."

"Oh sorry again." Betty went into thoughtful mode. The sudden clink of her cup on the patio table made me jump.

"You know Jean-Louis does have a younger brother, maybe…"

I raised my right hand policemen –like. Betty paused then went on, "Well yes, maybe not young enough."

I nodded. I had a mouthful of coffee now; I swallowed and let out a well meaning sigh in recognition of my dilemma.

"But look," she was determined to help. "Why don't you come out with the two of us tonight, just for a meal? You don't want to be here every time young Rudolf turns up. You don't want to seem erm…"

"Desperate, Betty, was that the word you were looking for?"

"Come on, you're letting this really get to you. Now stop it."

We had been together just days and already she seemed to know me better than anyone.

"You know you may have overlooked one very obvious possibility."

"What, that he is gay?"

"Well yes that would explain everything." Betty was triumphant with her solution. "Perhaps my dear daughter already knew this and forgot to tell us."

"Oh that's possible." The thought of course had occurred to me but somehow I didn't think so. However, it was a better outcome than just plain rejection so I decided to go along with it, for the time being.

"You're right Betty I will come out with the two you tonight but no foursome, do you hear?"

"Okay, okay."

Betty pushed back her chair the metal legs scraping the patio tiles. "I must go and have a little rest. Ever since my last stroke you know..." Betty smiled as she lolloped towards the French windows. I picked up a linen napkin off the table and threw it at her. She feigned distress as it reached its target.

"I'll tell," she shrieked and ran indoors.

"So will I," I countered, laughing.

What a character and I have met a few.

Betty told me, she had decided to have a slight stroke the moment Deirdre had suggested shipping her off to her other daughter in Brittany, while they did Italy. Betty had protested that she would not be able to cope with all the steps, when they got wet. And in any case Belinda has no patience with old people, not like you darling. I could just imagine Deirdre falling for that. So it was agreed that they would try and get someone to come and stay. She wasn't bad enough for a nursing home but a bit too frail to leave home alone. This had been Gerard's description at the interview. *If they could see her now.* I wondered whether I should take a few photos in case I needed them later on. A little light blackmail maybe... I mean once Deirdre and Gerard get back... maybe I could stay on...Me and Betty could get a small place together... who knows. Still, this was silly. They had only just left and were not due back until October. A lot could change in that time. Maybe I would get sick of the warm sunshine, wonderful food...Sights, sounds and smells, worth getting out of bed for. Ha!

****

Betty reappeared after her self- imposed siesta. It certainly seemed to work. Her two hour nap in the afternoon meant she was still, 'Up for it!' her latest favourite expression, at two a.m. Betty was widening her vocabulary by watching some of my videos. She particularly liked the American ones. Miami Vice for example. Such nice young men she pronounced, licking her lips.

Betty had produced a whole new wardrobe since D and G, as she called her daughter and son-in-law, had left for Italy. Especially jewellery and make up. So Betty arrives back on the patio wearing a flimsy see through blouse with strapless sequined bra underneath and black flowing trousers. She did a little pirouette to make sure I had the full view.

"Modom doesn't approve."

"Not surprised," I said getting up from a very languid state and collecting the coffee cups at the same time. "You've got a much better cleavage than your daughter."

"Ah Deirdre, that poor girl has a chest, always has had, no change since she was fifteen. But it's obvious that Gerard likes the Kate Moss look."

"Yes they do seem happy; suited even. I have to admit having met Gerard in London; Deirdre was the last person I envisaged."

Oops. I wondered if I had gone too far. It is one thing to slate your own children, quite another for someone else to do it, but Betty just laughed.

"But then I taught her well you know."

Numerous visions crowded my mind, none of which seemed possible to voice, even with my new found openness that Betty encouraged, so I said nothing. Betty was watching my expression.

She continued. "Pelvic floor exercises dahling and of course I gave her the Kama Sutra and all of Colette to read." Betty waited for my response.

"Me too. Colette I mean. I love her."

Betty just nodded as if it confirmed her suspicion.

"Sun over the yardarm yet?"

"Not a chance. Hours yet Betty."

"Oh well. It must be somewhere in the world. Got any of that Pimms left?"

"Yep. Fruit, umbrella, ice?"

"Have you known me to do things by half Laura?"

"Never. Coming up."

I somehow carried the jug, two glasses and a bowl of pistachios, from the kitchen onto the terrace.

"You could use a tray."

"I know, but they are all wicker and have a wobble factor."

"On top of the freezer there is a normal one. M and S; pastel flowers." Betty rolls her eyes.

"How did you get it up there?"

"I didn't, Jean-Louis did and I forgot to ask him to put it somewhere, where us elves can reach it."

"All good things…"

"Ha! Told Jean-Louis that one. I am improving his English by cliché."

"I thought you said he spoke English like a native?"

"He does but only text book stuff." Betty winked and smiled.

I changed the subject for fear of 'hearing too much information' again.

"He is bringing his car tonight Betty, isn't he? Jean-Louis I mean. He doesn't have a side car for that black beast does he?"

Betty spluttered as the last gulp of Pimms shot down her nose.

"Sorry Betty. You okay?"

Betty was crying, laughter tears, now. I grabbed a paper napkin off the table and handed it to her. The steady low rumble of Jean-Louis' Mercedes interrupted us.

He parked as usual at the end of the drive. He could see Betty dabbing her eyes, so he hurried towards us, scattering gravel and creating a dust cloud behind him. I felt guilty as I imagined what the dust would be doing to his navy YSL silk shirt and cream slacks. He ran his right hand through his resplendent thick black wavy hair. Betty told me he pulled out any grey hairs with tweezers.

"Ma puce. What is the matter?"

Poor Jean-Loius. He looked so concerned. Betty was incoherent. She could only look at Jean-Louis, then at his car and then start howling again.

"Laura?" Jean-Louis towered over me, hands splayed towards Betty.

Lion protecting his mate. "What is this...?"

"Oh Jean- Louis, I'm sorry. She is fine really..."
"Fine? What is fine?"

"Ah yes. Betty please stop. Tell him you are okay."

Betty waved both hands in front of her face in attempt to calm herself down.

She took a deep breath but started to giggle before she could talk.

"Okay. She could be like this for a while." I said.

Jean-Louis was now on bended knee by the side of Betty's chair. He was holding both her hands in his. Wow. This had to be the real thing. He would have to go home and change. I had never seen true love close up before.

Jean-Louis turned his head towards me. I continued.

"I said something funny. That is all. Nothing to worry about."

"Something about me?"

Oh god. The male ego. It was beginning to replace his concern for Betty. He thought we were laughing at him. Careful now Laura. Foot-mouth. Think...

Fortunately Betty saved the moment.

"Cheri. I am fine. It means okay. Okay? It was just this."

She grimaces as Jean-Louis stands up to reveal a left knee spattered with rust coloured dust.

He doesn't follow her gaze. Yep, it had to be true love. Maybe his brother...No, probably chalk and cheese. Another cliché for Jean-Louis, I thought.

"Right, now, listen."

Betty pats the seat next to her. Jean-Louis sits.

"Laura is coming out with us tonight, yes? "

"Si, si. It is...fine!"

Jean-Louis, the eager student.

"Well, she just asked if you were bringing your car? "

Jean-Louis' expression says it all. Non comprendi.

"Or, whether perhaps..." Betty's convulsions start again.

"Jeesus, Betty, spit it out before Jean-Louis calls an ambulance!"

"Sorry, sorry. Laura wondered if you might have a sidecar for the Kawasaki?"

Jean-Louis has his eyes scrunched up with an expression which unfortunately reminds me of Manuel in Fawlty Towers, when he doesn't understand what Basil is saying to him. Not helpful.

Betty and I glance at each other and collapse into peals of laughter. At the same time I realise we have made things ten times worse. He now knows we are not only laughing at him but at his beloved black beast as well. I am really afraid this is going to be too much for him and he will jump up and leave.

Betty will never forgive me. Although she is doing most of the laughing.

"Jean-Louis please. We are not laughing at you or your motorbike."

His eyes still screwed up, focus on mine. At this moment I feel for interpreters at the United Nations. One wrong word...

"I simply said, would you be coming in your car or do you have a sidecar for your motorbike? This is English humour Jean-Louis. It is called absurd, nonsense, stupidity. It is not malicious."

He looks mildly relieved. Curious instead of cross. Progress.

Jean-Louis looks at Betty for confirmation. She nods. Her laughter has subsided into hiccups. She absently reaches for her drink, momentarily forgetting that it is empty. Jean-Louis looks down at his left knee.

"Mais non!" he leaps up, almost knocking Betty out of her chair.

Betty is biting her bottom lip so hard I am afraid she might pierce it.

"We can go to the restaurant via your place Jean-Louis, so you can change." Betty managed to keep a straight face.

To our surprise, Jean-Louis apparently, suddenly got the joke. "A side-car for my Kawasaki?" His eyes were like saucers. The ones that go with teacups, not coffee cups.

"And we put Laura in it?" I wasn't sure I liked where this was going.

"What an idée Betty. I shall order one right away."

Sunday 2nd July.

Sur le Ringroad d'Avignon.

Betty is off with Jean-Louis for the day today. I am not sure where and I can't help but wonder if she knows it is the French Grand Prix at Magny Cours. It's too far from here for me to drive but perhaps Jean-Louis is going to treat her... I would love to go, or I could go and watch it in a cafe in Martigues. There are plenty with big screens these days or I could go to Jean Alesi's home town of Avignon and watch it in a cafe there. Seemed sensible to me.

So off I went to Avignon centre-ville in time for coffee. I walked through the archway, the one with the clock tower above, which opens out into a large typical Provencal Square. People scurrying with baguettes tucked under their arms, you almost felt you were watching a tourist video.

There were a couple of large cafes with televisions perched up on the wall. Okay if I was at the front or had no-one tall in front of me. Not easy when you are five foot two. I wandered out of the main square down a side street and found what can only be described as the local cosy cafe. High stools up at the bar and a large television protruding on an extending arm.

Now the real conflict. Lunch and the start of the Grand Prix. The cafe although ideal for watching the race was not going to provide much in the way of culinary delights. But I suppose it was worth putting up with a ham baguette for Jean Alesi.

It was twelve thirty when I settled myself at the bar by the television, already tuned to T F 1. Sometimes I think the preamble before the race is more interesting than the race itself. Magny Cours is in the centre of France, beautiful but I wouldn't have thought very accessible. I don't know what happened to the Paul Ricard circuit in Marseilles.

The barman places my ham baguette in front of me as I stare at the TV screen. He assumes I am going to support the English driver Damon Hill or even the Scotsman, David Coulthard. I soon put him straight. Jean Alesi? He questions me, amazed. So I explain I have come to his hometown to watch him. The barman tells me his garage is only around the corner. I wonder if any of his friends might pop into this bar but then they are probably at Magny Cours.

It was fun watching the race but even more fun watching the bar fill up and the barman telling bemused Frenchmen about the reason for the perched, middle aged, English woman and her passion for Jean Alesi. It's the eyes and the cheeky smile, I explained when asked.

Damon Hill won, with Jean Alesi coming fourth.

All I had to do now was to get home. Did I mention that Avignon has its own ring road, a peripherique, a one way system? Well it does. Over the next 40 minutes I covered all of it....three times. Driving into Avignon was simple, just follow centre ville. Leaving and heading home, not so simple. In the end I pulled up and asked directions from a man walking along the pavement.

He spoke very good English, mainly because he was Irish! He watched my eyes glaze over soon after his first three instructions. "Look," he said "My car is parked very near to the exit you need to take, so why don't I get in and direct you; then you can drop me off." He smiled. I smiled. We both reckoned we would be safe. He was as good as his word and I dropped him off. It wasn't until I got home I realised his sunglasses were still on the dashboard. I have them to this very day. So if you're an Irishman who was in Avignon on Sunday 2nd of July 1995 thank you and I'm sorry.

As it turned out Jean-Louis had not whisked Betty off to see the race. He had asked his brother to record it so he could watch it later.

****

ALL EXPENSES PAID

Ensconced on one of the padded sun-loungers, I had dozed off and the music had stopped. I came to and looked up and saw Ed creeping up the drive. He obviously realised that making me jump was not a good idea. As he walked towards me he tilted his head to one side. "Okay?" he said. The universal greeting that means so much. "Okay." I said. We both knew it was a lie. I had checked Ed's itinerary and realized he had a free day tomorrow. So no early breakfast. Hurrah.

I had moved onto my favourite drink, Jack Daniels and Coke. The bottles were still on the table. The ice bucket and the lone glass seemed to paint a picture he understood.

He walked into the kitchen and came back with a clean glass. He pointed at the Jack Daniels and then at himself.

"Feel free." I said. He frowned. So I merely nodded, it was simpler.

I held up the CD case of Elton John. He nodded. So I pressed play. I had only heard half of it anyway. And the day I have too much Elton John well...

Ed pours himself a drink. Picks up the ice bucket, swishes it around and retrieves a single piece of ice for his drink. He reaches into his pocket and pulls out a black leather wallet. Is he going to pay me for the drink? No, instead he plucks out a passport size photograph. He passes the photograph to me.

The photograph is certainly of a young woman and a child. The child sits on her knee and looks up adoringly at the woman. I glance at Ed and try to read his expression. I can tell nothing from the photograph but everything is in his face when he says the name. One I find hard to grasp. I will think of her as Katia. It will have to do. So many thoughts run through my head and none of them seem to be kind questions. Where do we go from here?

I hand the photograph back to him with a slight nod and hopefully a knowing smile. I raise my glass. He nods back and takes a drink. Ed leans back in the chair and closes his eyes. I decide to go and find 'my' photograph. When I get back downstairs he still has his eyes closed and Elton is still serenading us. I wait until the music stops with a click and Ed's eyes come open. I hand him a passport size photograph. A young man in uniform. It is not very clear.

I see the surprise in his eyes slowly replaced with understanding. He purses his bottom lip and nods and hands me back the photograph.

We clink glasses and say no more. The moment has passed. A part of me would like to know; girlfriend, wife, child but then I do not want to discuss my photograph, so maybe he feels the same.

Sometimes lack of language can be a blessing.

ALL EXPENSES PAID

Monday 3rd July

Letter from Ed.

The following morning it is nine-o-clock by the time I get downstairs. There is a note pinned up in the kitchen on the wall. It is from Ed and he obviously had help, as the English is almost, spot on.

Dear Laura and Betty

Thank you very much for your hospitality. I do not wish to offend either of you but a friend, he is staying nearby in the big house and they have plenty of room for me. I have made a copy of the tape of my favourite songs for you Laura. Hear it is. (There is an arrow pointing down to the counter, where sure enough a cassette tape sits. It is marked, compilation summer 1995.)

Hope to see you both at tomorrow's concert.

Ed's name is scrawled at the bottom. Still a mystery to me.

Dear Julia.

Ed, you know, the dancer guy. He's moved in with some friends. Can't blame him. We had a long chat. Who am I kidding? He showed me a photo of a young woman with a baby on her lap. I showed him my photo of my soul mate. Stop rolling your eyes. I know it is my fault. I did the right thing and it just turned out to be the worst decision of my life. Drama intended. :-0

Anyhoo. Ed leaves me a tape of his favourite songs. He spelt compilation right. I have managed to play one side so far. Talk about music to slash your wrists to. You know me and song titles, so here's some of the lyrics to give you an idea.

It must have been love, but it's over now. From a distance. *Think that one's Cliff.* A better place. Misjudged love. *Both Elton? Next the classic:* I can't live if living is without you. I miss you more than words can say. I'll stand by you. *I know, I should know this one!* Please forgive me, I can't stop loving you. Feels like the first touch. *Both Rodders, I think?* The winner takes it all. *Even I know that one!*

Okay, you get the idea. And no I didn't ask about the woman and the baby. Pictures, thousand words, bla bla.

Hey, great news about your new job with the local rag, sorry newspaper. You'll be perfect at selling advertising. No luck from me needed. Is this going to scupper your chance of popping over for a few days? Hope not.

Gotta dash. Sunshine calling.

Will give you a quick ring next week on my new phone. Did I tell you it's the Motorola Flip phone? Very MI6.

Ciao baby,

Me xxx

p.s Betty has given me some special tea bags to try. She says they are anti...something. Fat, hopefully. Let you know how I get on.

****

"So how was your day yesterday Betty?"

"It was lovely Laura thank you. Jean-Louis knows about this little restaurant. It is tucked away in the hills. Not far for from the Airport, not that you would never know it. It was so peaceful. Nothing too grand and the usual wonderful home cooked food."

"Sounds great. Jean-Louis coming round today?"

"No, he said something about having to do some tax papers by the end of this month. And as the garage doesn't open until two thirty, he said it would give him chance to get it done. And I saw the note from Ed, so at least you don't have to worry about fetching and carrying."

"Yes, let's face it, it is better all round. I guess you could hardly expect him to fit in, just like that. Oh and do you want to go to the concert tomorrow evening?"

"Not really to be honest; do you Laura?"

I shook my head slightly at the thought. We were obviously both feeling very lazy today. Not hard to do here.

We scoured the kitchen and discovered some Parma ham in the fridge. The bread van had been and I have returned with two very fresh baguettes. Betty had told me about the risk of having an English accent and been fobbed off with last night's bread. I had developed the knowing look that seemed to work. What we really needed was a wonderfully ripe cantaloupe melon, to complete our lunch. There is a steep and twisting lane that runs from the edge of the road at Les Collines down to the sea. At the top of the lane where it rejoins the main road there had been a fruit stall the last few days. It would only be a five minute walk so I told Betty I was off to investigate.

The apricots adorning the trees in the front driveway were fully formed but still not soft to the touch. They needed a few more days to ripen. I couldn't wait. It had been one of my real pleasures living with my Leicestershire cottage. My garden was also the farmer's kitchen garden. I only had to open my back door and I could pull up carrots, shake off the soil, give them a little scrape et voila! Only I could be walking through a Mediterranean Village in the height of summer daydreaming about the cottage garden in England. Sure enough the wooden stall had been set out in the lay-by. Galia and Cantaloupe melons were organized in wicker baskets. At that moment I hoped that never again, would I have to walk around a supermarket with a metal trolley, in search of something that might actually smell and taste the way it looked. Here, the aroma from the melons... it was enough to make you want to run and fetch the Parma ham, to eat it there and then.

****

"So where did you live exactly, in England I mean?"

"I was born in Leicestershire, a lovely village called North Kilworth. Haven't been back for years, I hope it hasn't changed too much."

"North Kilworth... you're kidding? You were born there Betty?"

"I was, but I haven't been back for a long time. Has it changed much?"

"I don't know but then I have only known it for the last three years but I don't think so. I went to see a flat there. It was on the third floor of a beautiful oak beamed cottage him, overlooking the bowling green."

"Oh my goodness. Do they still use it?"

"Oh yes. I went there on a Sunday morning and the ladies team were all decked out in white. It was like stepping into the past. Is it the same Betty, bowls and the game they play down here? They call it Petanque, don't they?"

"They do but I'm sure the locals would insist that it is a different game entirely."

Betty chuckled to herself.

"No good asking Jean-Louis either, not one of his pastimes."

"Talking of past times Betty...?"

"Nosey little madam aren't you?"

But Betty was smiling. "Okay. What do you want to know?"

"Nothing much, just what happened between being born in a Leicestershire village and now really..."

"Is that where you met Deirdre's father?"

"So hang on what happened to the flat you went to see? Too noisy for you, was it?"

"Ha ha Betty. No, it was really too small. Not enough space for all my books."

"So where are they now?"

"All boxed up and being stored in Julia's spare room."

"Now *she's* a good friend."

"She is, but *you* are changing the subject."

"Moi?"

I just nodded and made myself comfortable on my favourite green and white striped padded recliner. As usual my top half was beginning to glow nicely but for some reason my legs remained firmly, imitating milk bottles. So I strategically placed my legs in the sun and waited for Betty to start her tale.

"Okay," said Betty. "Once upon a time, twin girls were born. Margaret and Marietta on the 13th of May 1913. Margaret soon became Betty and she has a middle name Agnes which she absolutely hates and never allows it to be used."

Betty peered over the top of her sun glasses to make sure I got the message.

I raised both eyebrows and nodded silently.

"Betty met Bernard at the amateur cine club in Market Harborough. They had three passions; films, cycling and each other. Bernard was in the local church choir. Betty was never a church goer. Betty was thirty five when she became pregnant with Deirdre, which was considered seriously old back then. And to be pregnant and out of wedlock in 1948 was not a good thing. Betty and Marietta shared the family home. It was big enough to raise a family. Bernard had offered to marry Betty. It was the obvious thing to do but Marietta persuaded Betty not to do it. She and Betty would bring up the baby together. Bernard would have been a good father but most probably a lousy husband. They stayed friends but once the baby was born, Bernard moved to Surrey and they lost contact."

I started to wonder why Betty was telling her story in the third person. She was deep in thought now and I didn't want to interrupt, so I sat and waited.

"And then Marietta was taken ill and Bernard started to visit weekends. He was great with Deirdre but he had another life and I respected that. Deirdre was just two years old when Marietta died. Bronchial pneumonia. She was never physically strong. All the stuff you hear about twins. It's all true. There's hardly a day…"

Betty's voice began to falter the moment she mentioned pneumonia. I could hear the emotion welling up in her voice, as I felt tears prickling the back of my eyelids.

"She was just thirty seven…"

Betty sat up and shook her head slightly as if she could dislodge the thoughts.

"Ah Betty, I'm sorry…"

"It's OK Laura. Just somehow it never gets any easier. And of course I don't get to tell the story for the first time very often these days. Jean-Louis knows but he never asks unless I offer. He says he's happy to know who I am, now. He says the present Betty is more than enough for him!"

A slight glint and a twinkle had been restored. Betty sighs but her mouth is still turned down and sad.

I was about to ask about Deirdre and Gerard, when she continued.

"A year later I moved to Surrey and I got my own little flat near Bernard. Very different place; very different people. I couldn't bear living in the village where I had grown up."

Betty gives a little cough hoping to shake off the last stubborn emotion.

Her voice alters suddenly as she says. "I used to be a piano teacher you know, ballet and tap mainly, which I could do at home. And I worked part time in the Sue Ryder charity shop, twice a week, the one in Guildford. Everybody loved Deirdre she was such a good baby. Always smiling at everybody. I had no end of babysitters."

"Would you play the piano now Betty, if we went somewhere, where they had one?"

"Possibly. I'll suggest it to Jean-Louis. Get a crowd together, that would be fun."

Betty starts to get up from her chair. "Well there you are. A little potted history."

I was just sorry it had been such a painful story.

"Did you drive Betty?"

"Not in the early days but then I had the most wonderful car. Funny you should ask about it. Deirdre thinks I sold it ages ago. No power steering far too heavy bla bla . A friend keeps it in his garage takes it on the occasional run."

"Bernard ?" I asked

"Hmm. How did you know that?"

I shrugged, because I really didn't know. I felt it was time to change the subject.

"Deirdre was telling me that she met Gerard when she was touring with the netball team over here?"

Betty sat down again, obviously relieved that we had moved on.

"Yes Deirdre was at Manchester and Gerard was at Bordeaux."

"Don't tell me Gerard used to play netball?"

"Don't be ridiculous Laura. You have met him."

"True, I was only kidding. So he was a spectator?"

"Something like that. Strangely, they are a little bit cagey about how they actually met. Still; what does it matter as long as they're happy?"

"So they have been together quite a while. About five years, I think Deirdre was saying?"

"Yes, although, I didn't know about it for quite some time..."

I started to smile and Betty glanced across at me.

She said nothing but we both realised in some ways, mother and daughter, were quite alike.

"You've been here, how long now Betty?"

"Since November last year and I had the stroke the previous June. I mean really, I was getting on fine but the thought of another winter. And when Dolce and Gabanna suggested I come over for the winter with the idea of making it long term, I thought, why not?

Dolce and Gabanna, I chuckled to myself.

"The hardest thing was leaving Brandy behind."

I hesitated for a moment. I had only known Betty for a matter of days but I was pretty sure she was not talking about bottled kind.

"Brandy?" I asked innocently

Betty's smile had a slight tinge of disappointment.

"Brandy is my wonderful big Ginger cat. I left her with Audrey; she's my Julia."

"Dinner?" I suddenly said

"Not sure I like the fact that I mentioned my cat and then you said dinner?"

"No connection Betty I promise you, just suddenly felt hungry. What are we going to do tonight?"

"Well, we have been lazy all day..."

"So we could be lazy all evening as well?"

Betty raised her hand and we high fived.

Pasta with a Pesto sauce and salad. And a large slice of tarte aux fraises that had somehow managed to survive the weekend in the fridge. We had just settled down with a mug each, of green tea when the phone rang. Betty answered it and from the sounds and shrieks of laughter I had a feeling she was talking to Audrey. I'm glad the evening ended on a high note...

Time for bed.

Tuesday 4 July.

Free samples.

I wasn't sure at first but Martigues definitely has a certain charm. With its intricate waterways you can see why it is dubbed the Venice of the South of France. Although to be fair I have never been to Venice so I don't know whether it's really a fair comparison. It's a mixture of old and new. Quite a lot of property was built in the 1970s and has a Port Grimaud feel to it. Lots of pinks and pale greens and of course the red rooftops. But despite all this, my real reason for coming into Martigues today is to go to my favourite shop. I had been buying products from Yves Rocher for years. In England I used to order everything through a catalogue and couldn't have been more excited than when my new parcel arrived. Even in my teens I had a passion for all things French. And they certainly seemed to be ahead of the game; focusing on all natural products from sustainable areas. Environmentally friendly was their watchword long before anybody else. Then suddenly a few shops opened in the UK and I was able to go and browse but they didn't last too long, I don't know why. Always excellent value for money perhaps that was the problem, sometimes things just seem too good to be true. Then of course, along came the Body Shop and no one could deny the effect they had on a whole generation and their spending power.

Funny really, how even now, as I politely resist the assistant's attention, I think back to those first parcels and how the products I had ordered were never a disappointment, the real excitement lay in the bottom of the box. Flinging shower gel, moisturiser, lip balm on my bed, I plunged my hands into the white polystyrene shapes to recover sachets and tiny plastic bottles. A great way to try out the latest items. Perfume, after shave and my favourite, teeny weenie lipsticks, not much bigger than your thumbnail. They still give away free samples with your purchases in the shops but somehow it's not the same. Today I have come in to buy some body lotion. I am starting to get quite a nice colour already. It's true I am a sun worshipper but I can appreciate it from underneath the shade of a tree. I don't want to end up like a prune. Skin cancer may be a reality but the thought of being unnecessarily wrinkled worries me far more. And take Betty as an example, she has a healthy glow, a light bronze, and skin in wonderful condition.

I tell the assistant that my skin is sensible. Which is more than can be said for the rest of me. Try saying the word sensible with a French accent and what you have is the word for sensitive. Soap makes me itch, a lot of make-up does the same, so I stick with what I know suits me. The very young assistant assumes I am new to Yves Rocher. I try to explain, in my best French, that I have been a fan for over twenty years. She looks at me in disbelief. I kid myself that she must think I started wearing make-up when I was five.

I spot some lavender foot cream and decide to get it for Betty. She does her own manicure and by the looks of her feet, does her own pedicure too. She certainly knows how to look after herself. I walked back to the car swinging my nice new shiny carrier bag with all its goodies. I saw the assistant drop a few free samples into the bottom of the bag. That's good when I get home I can tip it all out on the bed and call Betty to come and see. Doesn't take much to make me happy.

While I was in Martigues I wanted to grab an English newspaper, get a coffee and possibly meet up with Pierre. He had given me 'the eye' the previous Saturday, when I was dropping Ed off. Hearing my accent he wasted no time in introducing himself, saying he was in need of English lessons and that he was in that cafe (he pointed to the one by the bus stop) most Tuesdays and Fridays. But first I found the newsagents who would let me buy the Sunday Times cheaper on a Tuesday. A bit like the English bread really. A little stale but better than nothing. I spotted Pierre as I was coming out with my newspaper. He was wearing a white T shirt and shorts, white ankle socks and trainers. He told me he was having an affair with a woman whose husband thought she played tennis every Tuesday. Seemed a bit extreme for him to dress the part as well. Maybe it made it easier for them both to lie. Whatever. I had sat down and ordered my coffee by the time Pierre spotted me. He sauntered over in his usual confident way. The Gallic shrug emphasized his raised eyebrows as he plonked himself down on the chair opposite me. He tilted his head back and caught the waiter's eye. A double expresso appeared within moments.

"Ca va?"

"Ca va." He agreed.

"So why so serious?" I asked.

"It's your eyes; they keep me awake at night."

"And how *exactly* do they do that?"

Pierre leaned across the table gathering both my hands in his. "I keep imagining how they must look when you reach a climax." He looked imploringly at me.

With only a hint of a smile I replied. "I'll take a photo next time it happens."

"You know that's not what I meant."

He let go of my hands and placed them round his espresso cup.

"Am I ever likely to find out?" He continued, seriously this time.

"I don't know."

It was an honest answer. There was something about him that made me hesitate, usually I could say yes or no but not this time. His dark eyes sparkled and his outdoor lifestyle meant he had a year round tan. He worked at the docks in Marseilles. He came into Martigues for a little gentle relaxation and a game of tennis with his mates. Ah, so maybe the husband is ...

"Well I'm off to play Boule; want to see how the experts do it?"

Pierre downed the almost certainly cold coffee in one gulp, sliding back his chair at the same time. I shook my head.

"Got to get back in time to see Betty before she goes out on her date."

I had told Pierre about my job.

"She sounds like quite a character; you should bring her with you next time you come."

Thinking that I'd like to know her reaction to Pierre I said I might just do that and pushed back my chair and retrieved my handbag from the floor. "Friday?"

" Friday," I agreed. "All being well."

"All being well," mimicked Pierre.

I was going to have to start charging for these English lessons. Not that he really needed them but his accent could do with a bit of work.

As he walked away I realised that the answer would be no. It wouldn't happen. Imagine him staring into your eyes waiting for that moment. Nope. Ah well. Plenty more poisson...

ALL EXPENSES PAID

Helen Ducal

Saturday 15th July

Midnight swim. Cossie optional.

Dear Julia, mon amie,

He was without a doubt the most gorgeous guy I've seen so far. I mean Thierry's cute and fun, but well, yes you guessed it...petit.

Now here at the local beach restaurant is a six foot tall, dark and extremely handsome waiter. The muscles, the tan, the beads of sweat on the brow by the end of a busy evening, all needed my very personal attention.

I've been going to the restaurant mainly during the day for a coffee or coke (the brown fizzy sort, don't worry), sometimes with Betty but last night I went for a meal. Thought it would give me longer to study my prey.

"Your mother not with you tonight?" asks, oh-so-handsome-one.

"Oh, no she's not my mother. I'm just her...what's the best word...housekeeper."

"Aah." This obviously made a difference; he visibly relaxed. "You have to work for her tonight?" he asked.

"No, I'm free." I wondered if I should add, willing and able, but I think he was getting the message.

"You like a midnight swim. You come back after your meal?"

"Oh yes, that would be lovely." I said in my best English, as if he had just asked me to visit the museum.

The fish soup was delicious. I can almost smell it now, just thinking about it...that lovely rich saffron colour, chunks of succulent white fish oozing with garlic, white wine and fresh parsley.

I soaked up the last drops with the last piece of crusty bread.

It was ten pm, perfect. Two hours to prepare. It was only a ten minute drive home.

Now what to wear...shorts and tee shirt...not going to spoil a good dress by getting sand all over it.

I arrived back at the restaurant at 12.10.

The place was still packed. No problem. I ordered a Calvados. I could wait...and wait...

It was 1.20 by the time he'd finished. He must be knackered I thought, purely selfishly.

"Got your swimming costume?" he asked.

"Damn, knew I'd forgotten something!" I said, holding the serious face long enough to confuse him. I soon put him straight.

1.30am, the Mediterranean...the moonlight...my first Frenchman...my first time in the sea...my...my...

When you coming over? You must be due some time off soon?

Speak to you at the weekend.

Bisous (kisses) Laura.

P.s. His name was Phillipe.

Sunday 16th July.

Jean-Louis is coming to take Betty out for lunch. He has a cousin visiting from Barcelona and he wants to introduce him to Betty. I start to wonder about this very unusual relationship. Jean-Louis's family knows about Betty but Betty's family knows nothing about Jean-Louis. Still, Betty must know her daughter and son-in-law well enough to know what she's doing. She obviously enjoys the clandestine aspect of it but I can't help thinking, what would Deirdre and Gerard's reaction be? Wouldn't they be glad that Betty had met somebody who made her happy? Wouldn't they secretly hope that Betty might move in with him? It was impossible to tell after seeing them for such a short time together, to know just how well their situation worked.

I decided to drive down along the coast and give Sausset les Pins, a try. Smaller in the sense that it had less shops and cafes than Carry Le Rouet but bigger in that it had a straight expanse of beach, some of it even had sand. I like watching the Grand Prix in a bar or cafe because let's face it, at times the race can be merely a procession. It's in those moments that you can survey the other customers and try and decide who supports whom. Of course it becomes abundantly clear when Schumacher overtakes for example, his fans rise from their seats and clap their hands. Doesn't mean they are German of course, just that they like the maestro's style. And now it's even more amusing as I found out in Avignon, to be a Brit supporting a Frenchman. By the end of the race my favourite driver with the gorgeous eyes had become a Brit sandwich. He came second after Johnny Herbert but pipped David Coulthard to the post.

This particular cafe was right on the beach but had a huge TV screen suitably angled to avoid the glare from the sun. Again my choice of eating place clashed with my Grand Prix viewing. On reflection I'm not complaining, who wants to go and have a wonderful three course lunch interspersed with vroom, vroom. I happily munched my way through an enormous pan bagnat. When the race got a little boring, I lifted the lid and removed the slices of raw onion, which I always forget to ask them to do. I love the rest; it's basically a salad Niçoise in a big, soft, round, flowery bun. Yummy.

There was general amusement along with a little confusion to my obvious favourable reactions to Jean Alesi. But one woman in particular, she turned out to be the owner of the bar, seemed to be watching me more than most. I had been an absolute devil and had a drink with my lunch. I had suddenly fancied a glass of red wine. It went down a treat. Now I was thinking of taking a stroll along the beach and then heading back. Watching the British Grand Prix had reminded me just how unreliable the weather can be there. And as I had the chance, I wanted to go for a walk and stay warm and dry. But the woman in question, her name was Veronique, seemed to have other ideas. She walked to the end of the bar where I was still sitting, with a bottle of red wine in her hand. She tilted the bottle and raised an eyebrow. I shook my head. I was going to stick to my one glass rule. She nodded. Un cafe? She asked. Why not, I thought. Veronique pointed to a table out on the beach. I smiled and walked over there. She brought my coffee and motioned to the chair opposite me. I nodded. She glanced back at the bar and her tall, dark, handsome partner smiled, grabbed a bottle of red wine and two glasses. Serge joined us. He spoke a little English and the three of us had a laugh about me supporting a Frenchman. With or without language it was clear what was coming next. Did I want to join them for the evening? They were having a private party. Not open to the public, they emphasized, in case I still hadn't got the message. Serge was running his large, hairy knuckled, right hand across the back of Veronique's neck. She was smiling leaning towards me, trying to gauge my reaction. Her long red hair fell to the one side. Serge grabbed handfuls and piled it up on top of her head. C'est jolie, n'est pas? I agreed it really suited her, very pretty. I explained that in a previous life (I have to stop saying that, I think the French take me literally) I had been a hairdresser. Serge immediately asked if I would cut his hair. This of course had nothing to do with him needing a haircut and everything to do with us making physical contact. I smiled at them both. I liked the idea in theory but I wasn't sure about the practice.

I told them I had to get back and maybe I would see them later. I grabbed one of their cards from the glass bowl by the till. I didn't really think I would need to phone them but I knew one day I would come across the card and smile at the memory.

****

When I got back the answering machine was blinking. Probably Deirdre checking up on us...in a good way. But then I thought maybe Betty was out and it was a message from her I'd better check. Julia's voice loud and clear reverberated around the tiny study. " Hello girls, Julia calling. Fancy a visitor next month? Hubby has an assignment nearby. Okay if I come and stay for a couple of nights? I'll arrive on Wednesday, the 9th of August if that's OK? Give me a ring as soon as you can. Need to book the flights. Hope you're all okay. Speak to you soon. Bye."

I didn't need to check with Betty I knew she'd love it. More's the merrier she would say.

I dialled Julia's number. I hoped she was in. I couldn't seem to find the redial button on the phone and dialling England has so many numbers. I was in luck.

"Hey you that's great news... Sure she'll love it no problem... She's out somewhere at the moment...Can you only stop two nights?.. Ah well. It will be hot you know... Yes August in the south of France pretty obvious really. Okay. Everything alright with you?.. Hey that's good... I've just got one more letter to send you. I'll do it tomorrow. The rest I can tell you when you get here... Brilliant. Give me a quick ring when you've got your flights booked and let me know what time I need to come and meet you?"

It was the following Saturday when Julia rang to confirm the dates and the time of her arrival. We kept the call short as Julia's husband pointed out, we would be seeing each other soon and there was really no need to increase British Telecom's profits. He was only half joking.

I promised Julia one more letter, so, I grabbed my diary, a fresh sheet of paper and a pen. There was half a bottle of wine in the fridge. I was sitting on the terrace when I remembered Betty had told me. 'Anytime you want to enjoy the sunset you just go and sit on my balcony, you don't need to ask.'

If she came back in through the inside staircase I would call out to let them know I was there or else I would see her arrive. We hadn't quite got the stage where you hang a sock on the bedroom door when you have company, but it may come to that.

A pink tinged sky peeking out from the back of the house was too much of a temptation so I clambered up the outside stairs and let myself in to Betty's pad and onto her balcony. I surveyed the garden. Three Oleander trees, three different colours. Cream with pink tinged edges to their flowers. A hot pink and a deep burgundy, my favourite. So beautiful. So deadly. Apparently just one leaf would be enough to kill you. I had to wonder if Agatha Christie had

ALL EXPENSES PAID

ever used this particular poison. The few white clouds turned pink as the sun set over the hills. Dusk can be quite a rapid affair here and I didn't want to bother with lights so, I wrote my letter to Julia while I could still see.

Helen Ducal

Dear Julia,

Great that you're coming over. Can't wait. I won't plan too much, expect you'll have your own ideas about what you want to do ;-)

So, let's see, what's happened the last few days? Here's an update.

Mon 17th July.

Went for a lovely walk this morning, before it got too hot. Bumped into a girl pushing twins in a buggy. Or is that a buggy with twins in it? Honestly she was as thin as a rake. How do these French women do it? Her name was Adrienne. Funny isn't it, we had only spoken for 10 minutes but she told me her name straightaway. In England you could talk to somebody for half an hour and still not know who they were. When she heard my accent she told me she loved porridge and marmalade. None so queer as folk, eh dragonfly?

Tuesday 18th. Went to the pictures. Saw Carrington. Unrequited love and all that. Not a laugh a minute. You'd hate it.

Friday 21st. Aix en Provence festival today. Took lots of photos. It is the most idyllic town. Just the right size. On our 'to do list' when you come over.

Saturday 22nd. I was woken up at five o clock this morning. Nothing tall dark and handsome. Reckon we've got squirrels or mega- mice in the loft.

Mon 24th Dug out one of the videos tonight to watch. Into the west. A real weepy. Think you'd like this one.

Thursday 27th Decided to go to a photography exhibition in Marseilles. Henri Cartier Bresson. Unfortunately while I was admiring his handiwork someone was fiddling with Beryl. Or to be more precise, the lock. They hadn't

ALL EXPENSES PAID

succeeded in getting into the car but then neither could I. I had to open the passenger door and climb across. Great . That's the last time I drive into Marseilles. Anyway it's a Renault Five for goodness sake, shouldn't be too much of a problem to get it fixed. But it is almost August. And I see so many local businesses are closed.

Pity Jean- Louis has an Alfa Romeo and not a Renault garage.

Sat 29th. Went to my usual cosy cinema. Saw Indochine *with Catherine Deneuve. Brilliant. Betty being wined and dined of course tonight. She is getting more action than I am. Did I tell you I went back to Philippe's restaurant but either he stopped working there or he was hiding in the kitchen when he saw me coming. Ha!!*

So there you go, that's it for now. Except, did you hear there was a bomb in the Paris metro on Tuesday? ☹

Hopes all is well in Blighty.

See you soon.

Au revoir ma petit chou. L xx

Tuesday 1st August.

One for the money.

It is Tuesday, the first day of August and I finally managed to tune my radio into the BBC World Service. Newspapers are all very well but who wants yesterday's news? I hadn't realised how much I liked knowing what was going on in the world. Isn't it often the way; you don't know what you're going to miss, until you miss it. Betty says the world can carry on quite nicely without her. She said living through the thirties and forties meant she had had her fill of news. If only they'd come up with some good news occasionally but no, it's all doom and gloom. She had a point, but as much as I loved my new home I liked occasionally to have background chatter in English. But all that would have to wait a while. I was sick of clambering over my passenger seat to get in to my car.

The Renault garage was just opening up when I arrived at nine thirty. I was lucky it was open at all. After all, this was now August in France, which equals closed, in many places. Congé annuelle. The yearly holiday. Sacred. Quite right too...once they've fixed my lock, I'll help them pack. The usual scratching of heads and perplexed looks that I had now come to expect, when I try to speak French, were alleviated by the arrival of the chef. As in, the boss, not somebody who cooks. He speaks enough English for us to communicate. He peered at the lock on my Renault Five, tapped his nose and disappeared into the back of the garage. He returned shaking his head. He implied that the lock had not arrived. It must be difficult to find a lock for a Renault Five in France. (I didn't say this out loud) He said he had ordered it three days ago. But then three days here is like three hours in the UK. Patience; if only it was one of my virtues. The boss disappears into his office and I can see him on the phone. C'est après midi? This afternoon? He mouths at me through the glass. Oui. I nod. They will be closed for lunch of course, probably until two thirty. I could go back at three- o-clock but four would probably be safer.

It is four thirty and I am leaning against my car in the Renault garage, waiting for the new lock to arrive. My usual smile has been replaced by a scowl and I have my arms folded across my chest. My strappy, turquoise, calf length cotton dress is practical in this heat. I had changed out of my shorts. Car mechanics find it impossible to work (even replacing locks) when they have distractions. A small vivid yellow van screeches to a halt. The black lettering on the side is reassuring. Ah. Renault parts delivery. At last.

Nice young delivery guy steps out of the van. He tries to saunter across the yard in his royal blue overalls but doesn't notice the metal ring bolted into the ground by the garage door. Were they used for tying up horses? I have noticed them by cafe doorways too. I will have to ask D and G when they get back. Or maybe Jean-Louis would know. Lost in thought for a second, I failed to point out the offending article to the nice young man. He tripped and sent his precious cargo flying into the air. Instead of trying to break his fall, I shot my hand out and caught the package. I was going to get my lock fixed, if it was the last thing I did!

To take the old lock out and put the new one in, took fifteen minutes. The paperwork took another fifteen. The lock cost one hundred and fifty Francs. The boss of this three man outfit was called Charles. It was embroidered on his overall pocket. Charles took a pen from behind his ear and scratched his bald head with it. He was trying to decide how much to charge me for labour. I could see the cogs whirring away. I stood my ground. Not flirty, not defensive. I gave him my best 'don't even think about it' look. He had the pen poised over the bill. I asked him if he would let me have one of his cards, as I intended to stay here for at least a year. A lot can go wrong with a R5 in twelve months.

He nodded, handed me a business card and wrote, labour: 50 francs and singed it with a flourish. I smiled politely as I tried to hide my amusement. I handed over 200 francs and waved to the nice young delivery man who was sitting on an upturned oil cylinder, with an icepack on his forehead.

Thursday 3rd August.

The forecast is for a real scorcher. The only time for someone as fair as me to be safely on the beach is before eleven a.m. and after five p.m.

Betty says she is happy to stay in the house and have a lazy day. She has started reading the book I leant her. She had watched me giggling to myself as I was reading it. I'll have that when you've finished, she said. I had remembered reading a write up somewhere. The author had won an award and with a name like Janet Evanovich, it was hard to forget. *One for the Money* was now firmly in my top ten books. Betty and I compared favourite authors the other night. We had already agreed on Colette but found that we both liked the short stories by de Maupassant. And neither of us has liked fairy tales as a child. Deirdre had loved *Alice in Wonderland*, which quite frankly completely freaked me out, but I loved science fiction. *Day of the Triffids*, Betty and I both said, at the same time. I pulled down the sleeve of my right arm, made my hand disappear, and then waved it about, making disgusting sucking noises. Betty looked at me and said, thank goodness Jean-Louis is not here. Explanation of this one, could take hours. I asked Betty how things were going. She seemed a little despondent today. Nothing that knocking off twenty years wouldn't cure. Betty, I admonished. You're talking like an old person, stop it immediately. She laughed and I grabbed her by the shoulders, pulling them up and then let them drop. I know, I know, she says and grabs the book and turns to go indoors. Then reminds me. Don't forget to be back by three-o-clock. We have the shiatsu lady coming, remember? She spends about forty five minutes making you feel ten years younger. Perhaps I should ask her for a double session.

I wandered down to the nearest beach at ten-o-clock, passing the food van on the way. I grabbed a bottle of water and went down to the tiny cove. A lone fisherman sat on a rock. Hard to believe this was August. But then the path was quite steep and shingle is not everybody's idea of a perfect beach. I managed to find some shade and scrunched up my towel to provide a cushion.

I opened my new book. It was going to be hard to beat Ms Evanovich but Rose Tremain soon had me locked into her world.

Sunday 6th August.

Saved by Priscilla.

"One of those days is it?"

Betty had come downstairs as light footed as ever and was standing in the kitchen doorway when she asked the question.

"That obvious is it?" I said.

"Well you certainly don't seem to be your usual self this morning. Have you had breakfast Laura, can I get you anything?"

This brought a smile to my face as I pondered for the umpteenth time just who was looking after whom. "Want to talk about it?" Betty asked.

I shook my head. "I honestly don't find it helps. What shall we do today?"

Betty appeared from the kitchen carrying her small breakfast tray. Fresh orange juice, sliced mango, yoghurt and a blueberry muffin. My eyes darted across to the muffin.

"I'll get a knife." Betty exaggerated a sigh.

I grabbed the coffee and helped Betty eat her muffin.

"I'm glad you found that new supermarket near the station. Nice to have a change from the croissants, pain au chocolat, baguettes... A hard life here isn't it Laura?"

"Going to be even harder to leave it Betty."

"Is that what's troubling you petal?" Betty's accent took on one of Irish undertones. It didn't quite work but she was trying to cheer me up and for that she could only be applauded.

"Not seeing Jean-Louis today?"

"No, we really wanted to break the pattern. In any case, absence only makes the heart grow fonder."

"Treat 'em mean keep 'em keen."

"Something like that Laura. So what do you want to do? Anything on at the pictures?"

"Hang on," I said through a mouthful of muffin. "I will go and get the local paper."

"Found it," I called from the kitchen.

"Well done," Betty called back, with thinly veiled sarcasm.

"Not the newspaper, I mean I found the perfect antidote to my malaise."

"You going to start using posh words again Laura?"

I just laughed and carried the paper in to show Betty.

"Here, look." I said and pointed to the evenings listing in Carry-le-Rouet.

"I've seen this once before and believe me it got me out of a far worse mood than this one. I was in Paris looking after an American lady."

Betty opened her mouth to come out with the pun that I was expecting, saw my raised eyebrows and closed her mouth.

"Yes unfortunately this American in Paris turned out to be an alcoholic, chain smoking, manic depressive."

"So I'm a piece of cake then?" Said Betty smiling

"You have no idea Betty. So what do you think?"

"*Priscilla, Queen of the Desert?*"

"That's the one. You will love it. I'm sure of it. What time does it start?"

"Six thirty. Shall we go down to Le Carry about five thirty for a little drinkie-poos?"

"Okay Betty, you can stop now. I'm feeling much better you don't have to try and entertain me. We will definitely go for a wee drink before the film." I tried out a Scots accent. It wasn't much better than Betty's Irish one…Why did we do it?

Betty took the breakfast tray into the kitchen and was loading the dishwasher as I started to go back upstairs.

"Oh Laura I nearly forgot. Jean-Louis says to tell you that the kiosk near the station now gets the Sunday Times, wait for it, on Sunday afternoon!"

"Did he say what time?"

"Laura we are still in France. Please don't ask the impossible."

"Sorry," I laughed. "Shall we reconvene at five pm?"

"We certainly shall and don't forget a shawl or a cardi or something. You know how they overdo the air conditioning in the cinema."

"Righto Betty. A tout a l'heure."

"Yep. Catch you later alligator," said Betty as she slammed the dishwasher door closed.

I lay on my bed and allowed myself a few fond but fleeting memories. It would not do, to dwell too long. Whoever said... It is better to have loved and lost than never loved at all? I could cheerfully strangle them at this moment. I could not help but wonder if I had paid the ultimate price for doing the 'right thing'. Only time would tell. Julia had said all along. It's your head or your heart Laura. You have to choose. I wondered if this date was clanging bells in his memory bank too. We both knew, that afternoon in the hotel would be our last. Both our heads had come to an agreement. The timing was all wrong. If only we had met twelve months earlier. This isn't a straight fight, Laura. Julia had been right. Just me and his other half. Let the best woman win, but when there is a baby...Too much at stake. We closed our chapter on Sunday 6th August. But the passion lives on, taunting me, reminding me. My head and my heart seem to be concluding that I may have made a huge mistake.

I rolled onto my side and picked up my new book. This would help. As soon as I had been able to read (I don't remember how old I was) it had been my constant solace. Especially comics. I loved the Beano and the Dandy. Couldn't be doing with the girlie ones. By that I mean, magazines for girls, not the top shelf variety. That came a lot later...

I jumped as the phone rang. It was Deirdre just checking that all was well. It was two thirty so I could say Betty was having her nap. Deirdre went off into one of her, 'oh silly me,' routines. I hoped she wouldn't suggest phoning back this evening. Although there was no reason why we shouldn't go to the cinema, I couldn't be bothered to think of another film we might see. I doubt Deirdre would consider a film about two drag queens and one transsexual in Australia,

ALL EXPENSES PAID

going off into the outback to entertain the locals, a suitable film for her delicate mother!

Wednesday 9th August.

Julia comes to stay.

Betty is totally addicted to the soundtrack from *Priscilla Queen of the Desert*. Her exercise routine is now even more hilarious to behold. She not only dances to the music, she actually re- enacts some of the scenes. I was dispatched on Monday morning to go into Marseilles, if necessary, which it was, to buy the video. *Fnac* said they could order it for me. I said they'd better. At least they *did* have the soundtrack on tape.

Deidre had phoned again on Monday to say that she had organized a surprise for her mother. Plus Deirdre thought I might like a couple of days' break. She had no idea how well we would get on together and had been thoughtful enough to arrange this for both of us. The taxi was due at ten a.m. It was now ten to ten and Betty was still sporting her favourite lavender leotard and shrieking *I Will Survive* at the top of her voice.

"What have I done?" I shouted across the music.

"You have created a monster Laura. Only you can be held responsible. I've told Jean-Louis about the film and he shuddered. Strange how insecure men can be. But I suppose I expected that reaction really. Not my tasse de thé, he said." Betty rolled her eyes and stabbed the stop button on the cassette player.

I glanced up at the clock on the wall. The one that Betty had placed there as soon as the kids, as she called them, had left. It was a big, smiley, green frog. Its arms told the time and its eyes went side to side, beating out the seconds. It would go back into Betty's room when they came back. It was as near as she got to re-creating the fun atmosphere that was obviously once her home. Just the kind of thing Deirdre found impossible to cope with.

"I'm really sorry I'm not going to meet Julia, but what can we do? Deirdre has paid for this midweek special at the Thalasslotherapy Spa, so I must go."

"Course you must, don't be silly. Here comes your taxi. Let me take your bag, in case he reports back to Deirdre."

"You think of everything Laura. Have fun with Julia. And if you need anything from my pad, just help yourself. See you Friday evening."

I felt a sudden pang. I was going to miss Betty. I rushed over and gave her a hug just as she was getting into the taxi. Betty smiled and when she was sure the taxi drivers' back was turned, she winked at me. He put Betty's bag in the boot and drove off at a leisurely speed.

Julia's flight was due in at Marseilles, at four thirty. She was taking two days out of her trip to the Camargue with her husband Martin. He was going to be photographing the wild life. Birds and horses, mainly. Julia and Martin seemed to have the perfect marriage. They did lots together but they also allowed each other space. Julia admitted she enjoyed looking at Martin's photographs once they were in an album, but somehow couldn't get excited about the actual taking of them. He takes so long, Julia had moaned to me one day. So it was agreed Martin would spend the first two days of the holiday checking locations and subjects, then by the time Julia joined him, he could snap away quickly. They would be arriving at the airport together but then he was hiring a car. I would pick Julia up, take her back to mine and then Martin would come and pick her up on Friday morning. So we would have two evenings and all day Thursday together.

She wasn't difficult to spot. Her enormous Louis Vuitton brown and cream suitcase, fortunately on wheels, seemed to be big enough to house her entire summer wardrobe. She pretended not to see me. This may have had something to do with the fact that I was brandishing a cardboard sign with the name Dragonfly on it.

****

"Oh my God, barbequed langoustines with garlic mayonnaise and the freshest, crustiest baguette, ever. Can you die from a pleasure overload? Which one is Phillipe?" Julia managed to talk and eat. Something I still struggle with. I love salad and so I live in constant fear of opening my mouth to reveal green teeth or gums.

"Don't think he's here anymore..." I looked round the restaurant. Nope, nowhere to be seen.

"You didn't...?"
"No, Julia. He was alive and well, when I last saw him. He managed to get on his motorbike ok."

"Motorbike? I thought you said you..." Julia looks round to see if anyone is within earshot. French restaurants , even the busiest ones, seem to have a gentle hum, not the ear-splitting rumble that passes as background noise in English restaurants. "In your letter you said..."

"Well, we started off in the sea. Just over there actually." I flung my right arm out; pointing my knife over Julia's left shoulder. She didn't bother to turn and look. They hadn't erected a sign.

"And then?"

"And then he followed me home. He said he wanted a shower."

"Good grief, such energy." Julia was smiling.

"Yep, we did it in the shower, after pausing at the kitchen table."

"Euw. Hope you've given it a good scrub since then?"

"You're such a germaphobe. Don't worry, I gave everywhere the once over in honour of your visit."

"So you can't see him?"

"No Julia. He probably doesn't work seven days a week and I'm not going to ask."

Julia pouts. "What about Axel, have you heard from him?"

"No, but he probably thought I was likely to turn him down again, so don't expect I will."

"So, it's really working out with Betty?"

"Oh Julia, she is brilliant. Shame she is away. She really gives me hope."

"Growing old disgracefully?"

"Absolutely."

We have cleaned every last morsel from our plates and the waiter, more Manuel than Phillipe, has returned with the dessert menus. I opt for the tarte aux fraises and Julia, true to form has the crème brulee. We both have coffee as we are unlikely to go to sleep anytime soon.

"New dress?"

I have been meaning to ask since we left the house. Julia manages to make the simplest dress look classy. It's a lovely soft lemon, looks like silk. A boned, strapless top, falls into soft pleats from just below the waist. Lemon and gold strappy three inch heels add to her catwalk look. At five foot nine, she is the same height as her hubby so she doesn't wear heels very often. He says he doesn't mind but Julia insists she knows different. Naturally it doesn't matter a jot to me. We are so different; we have never felt the need to compete. I was wearing my new blancmange pink tee-shirt dress with COOL written across my boobs. Pink espadrilles completed my casual look.

"You like?" Julia asked.

"Very Cote d'Azur, dahling. Shall we go?"

Julia nodded.

****

"You have my bed and I'll sleep in the spare room."

"The one that Ed used? With the tiny bed?"

"It'll be fine." I smiled

"We've shared before and this looks like a Kingsize?"

"If you're sure? Probably be more comfortable."

"Just remember, I'm not Phillipe or any others you haven't told me about?"

"And I'm not Martin!"

"True, you don't snore."

"We better get to bed. Lots to see tomorrow."

"Night sweet pea..."

Thursday 10th August

Grace Kelly under the stars.

It seemed strange not to be greeted by Betty's cheery morning banter but Julia soon made up for it.

"Look what I have just spotted!"

"A winning lottery ticket?"

"Not quite but it is the tenth today?" Julia frowned.

"All day..."
"And evening I hope. Look, *To Catch a Thief*, is on at... where is En plein air?"

"It means in the open air. Does it say Rouet plage?"

"Yep. Is it far?"
"No problem. What time does it start?"

"Twenty one hundred hours, boss."

"Ah yes, as the sun goes down. So that's this evening sorted. You calling Martin today?"

"What and have his phone disturb his twitching?" Julia peered over the top of *La Provence*. "I know you know what that means Laura..."

I shrugged and gave up the idea of hurtling myself into a full twitching session around the kitchen. Note to self: get new friends so I can use old jokes or find new jokes.

We had a lovely day, driving along the coast, stopping every twenty minutes or so. Julia wanted to take in the view. She couldn't believe how unspoilt it all was. "It hasn't been built up in the same way as its expensive neighbours along the Cote d'Azur. A lot of it has to do with the oil refinery at Fos-sur-Mer. On a bad day, you know it's there. Weird smell but doesn't usually last too long."

"Proper little tour guide, aren't you."

"One does ones best. It helps with the tips later..."

Julia rolled her eyes. I had to start looking for new jokes.

We had stopped for lunch in Martigues. Steak and frites at a lovely quayside cafe. Then we grabbed a seafood platter to share at home this evening before we went out. Julia marvelled how much choice there was when it came to buying ready prepared, fresh food. You'd never need to cook again if you lived here all the time...Julia glanced at me and knew she was echoing my dream.

We got back about five thirty and there was a message from Betty. Well I say it was from Betty but it wasn't her voice, to start with. I pressed play on the answering machine. Both Julia and I recognised the opening line of *I Will Survive* being played full blast. It was followed by a giggle as it abruptly stopped. 'A demain'. A voice said. And then another giggle and the line went dead.

"Betty?" asked Julia.

"Oh yes, that's Betty okay. A demain is..."

"Means tomorrow. I do remember some of my school girl French."

ALL EXPENSES PAID

Julia went to use the bathroom first. "How do you get this frigging shower to work? Lauraaaaaa."

I suddenly felt better about assuming Ed wouldn't know how to work it. Ha! "Coming ma petit chou."

With the shower running at a moderate temperature I went into my room to cleanse my face. I suddenly had the urge to clean my teeth, so I turned on the cold tap over my basin. A little too forcibly it seemed, as a scream from Julia made me realise that the water pressure had been affected in the bathroom. Betty had always used her bathroom upstairs and was on a different tank. Ah well. C'est la vie. I was even beginning to have pointless thoughts in French. Julia was clad in an enormous white fluffy towel. I didn't remember seeing it before. Had she been rummaging in D and G's room? Not really her style but it was not the towel I had given her yesterday. She saw my expression. "Brought this one with me. You know how I like my own things."

"Sorry about the change of water temperature." Don't joke, I warned myself. "Oh, it wasn't just that." Julia unwrapped the bottom half of her towel. Talk about lobster thighs! "Got any after sun cream?"

I felt guilty. I hadn't reminded Julia about suntan lotion. But I had thought, if I do, she will say 'Yes mummy'.

Sometimes you just can't win. We devoured the seafood platter, without any problem. Julia took a photo of it. She even enjoyed the little bulots that you need to coax out with a pin. She'll be eating veal next, I thought, but didn't say. We could have walked to where the film was being shown but the walk back would probably kill us. I keep forgetting to look at the gradient but there is a sign at the side of the road reminding you to use your gears, meaning, stay in low gear. To walk back up would be like climbing Everest but without the snow.

****

The film, of course was magical, somehow more so, watching it on the beach in the South of France. "Hard to believe it's almost thirteen years since we lost Grace Kelly..."

We were walking back to the car when Julia voiced what I had been thinking.

"And you know the spot where they stop the car, in the film?"

"With that spectacular view? Don't tell me...Is that the same road?"

"According to the papers."

We both let out a heavy sigh.

Friday 11th August.

Saying it with flowers.

I drove Julia into Martigues so we could meet up with Martin. Part of me hoped that Pierre would be in our usual cafe. After no sighting of Phillipe, my reputation was slipping. I needn't have worried.

"Lauwa!" Pierre's accent seemed thicker than ever. "And oo is ziss?"

Julia was looking her ever smart self. Cream linen trouser suit and peach coloured strappy top. She had the jacket slung round her pink shoulders. Her lustrous dark locks were caught up high on her head with a tortoiseshell comb. Pierre looked at me as if I had presented him with an early Christmas present. His ménage a trois fantasy would soon interrupted by Martin. The normally, cool, laid back to the point of comatose guy, that I had always known, suddenly became protective cave man.

Martin, unfortunately didn't know about Julia's sunburn on the tops of her arms. In a matter of seconds, Martin grabbed his wife by her shoulders, Julia screamed and Pierre glared at me and shot into the cafe next door.

All was soon explained and I went to retrieve Pierre who was hiding behind a newspaper at the bar.

It was all hellos and goodbyes in the space of twenty minutes. Martin had parked in a thirty minute zone. Ah, so that's who those spaces were for. I had been here long enough, to never, ever consider using anything less than two hours. What's the rush..?

Julia and I managed to get all teary eyed and Martin laughed. "You'd think you were never going to see each other again."

"Don't!" We said in one breath. He loved winding us up about our superstitions, as he called them.

I waved them off and promised to keep up the weekly letters.

When I got home there was Jean-Louis, appearing from the back of the house. "Ah Lauwa!" I could get used to this. It sounds so much better with a French accent. "Surprise." He says and points up to the top floor and Betty's pad.

"Okay." I mouth at him, as he already has his crash helmet on.

He raises both thumbs to me, hops on his bike halfway down the drive and roars off.

Curious being my middle name I sauntered round the back to see if I could get an idea what he had left for Betty. After all, it should be visible. As far as I knew he didn't have a key.

Oh, it was visible all right. My goodness, what a romantic. Shame I didn't fancy his brother but Jean-Louis said Paolo knew the language barrier would be too difficult. Phew, that nicely got me out of that one.

Betty was due back anytime. I couldn't wait to see her face.

I was in my room when I heard the taxi pull up. I was downstairs, quick as a flash. The driver was still hauling Betty's bag and the three carriers out of the boot. Betty went to pay the driver and he waved her away. Apparently Deirdre had even paid for the taxi in advance. I must stop having mean thoughts about her. I scooped up all the bags and put them just inside the living room.

"But I might as well take them straight up Laura. Did you miss me? How was Julia?"

"True, yes and fine."

Betty frowned as she went over my answers."Ah, yes. Well come on."

ALL EXPENSES PAID

She bent to pick up her bags. So I stopped her.

"Betty I think you will have to come back for those in a minute. Come and see..."

I led Betty by the hand to the rear of the house and her outdoor steps.

"Oh my God!" said Betty, clasping both hands over her face. She turned to look at me.

"I know. Do you think it is too late to have him cloned?"

Normally Betty would have been asking me to define cloned, but she was too busy stretching her neck, peering up to her top step. Jean-Louis had placed flowers on every one of the thirty two steps. All her favourites. Gardenias, yellow roses....I would tell you the rest but I don't know half the names of them. And not just one flower per step; some had a spray of six. And looped through her door handle was a bird of paradise.

Saturday 19th August

Reminiscing.

"So you didn't fancy tonight then Betty?"

"No. Anyway, I think it'll be an all nighter."

"And he's gone with his brother?"

Betty creased her brow. "Meaning?"

"Oh nothing. I was just thinking out loud."

"Sorry Laura, I just feel too lucky sometimes. Why me? He could have for someone so much younger..."

"Only on paper."

"Thanks Laura. Feel like a bottle of rosé?"

"Sure do, I'll get the glasses."

****

It was a truly rare evening. We both felt uncomfortable. There was only one thing for it.

"Now I think I'm going to turn in. Try as I might this heavy mood just won't leave me. See you in the morning Sweet Pea..."

ALL EXPENSES PAID

Betty gave me a half hearted wink and as she took the empty Rose bottle by the neck and headed for the recycling bin, round by the back door. Jean-Louis was emptying it regularly for us, in case the young 'uns came back unexpectedly.

Sunday 20th August.

Concert in the parc. No ticket? No problem.

I remember as a child being told about the concept of the 'white' lie. I don't recall there being any other colours available. However, I also remember being told, always tell the truth for your lies will find you out. This next chapter is really my attempt at a confession. I lacked a Catholic upbringing so this is my first opportunity. Perhaps some reader can come up with a suitable penance. Here goes.

Betty was spending the weekend with JL and his brother somewhere in the Pyrenees. Ideal now that the temperatures were well into the 30 degrees, day and night. We had left a message on the answer phone in case Deirdre rang, explaining our trip to hills, to cool off. Again. Oops. More white lies.

I had seen the concert advertised in the local paper. It was as much about the setting as the music that appealed to me. It was in the grounds of a beautiful chateau in La Roque d'Antheron. I had the idea of just turning up and buying a ticket, until I mentioned this to Pierre (the one with the eyes request) at my local cafe. It will be sold out, ages ago he said. At times like this I take on the mantle of a five year old being told they cannot have any sweets. I mentally grizzle, but I want to go, I hear myself say. Well they might have some returns; you could always just go and see on the night, he suggested. So I did.

To drive there you have to negotiate narrow, twisting roads with the possibility of falling rocks to your left and a sheer drop down a craggy ravine to your right. Fab... but what scenery. Pity my heart is in my mouth and my grip on the steering wheel is not enhanced by the nervous sweat, accentuated by the balmy

ALL EXPENSES PAID

temperature outside, although it is dropping as I climb. My R5 does not have air conditioning and I don't have the roof rolled back as, although there is no forecast of rain, the few sudden downpours that we have had made me decide against the odds of finding somewhere suitable to stop and put the roof up, should the unexpected precipitation, such a posh word for rain, occur. I am one of life's planners. I like to be organised. So, I have a new map of the area. A lot of road names and numbers have changed over the years. Very helpful. I have a rug in the car, a bottle of water, very lukewarm by now, and a torch. All in case I breakdown. I have my new mobile phone but the chance of getting a signal, where I am going tonight, zilch.

Very organised that's me. Betty has often commented on it. So, the fact that I am heading into the hills (aka small mountains) on a Sunday (nothing open) evening with a petrol gauge that is nudging red is not like me at all. I console myself with the fact that, as there will be loads of people in La Roque there will probably be a petrol station open. I have been here three months and I still expect the impossible!

My next thought consoled me with; Ah well, you can coast all the way back down, in neutral. I can hear my driving instructor turning in his grave. And no, I did not kill him. He died of natural causes. He was just very old when I learnt. For a split second I contemplate turning back, there and then, before it gets dark. Wuss. My adventurous side winning as usual. So, I continued.

As I drove into the village, I was glad. A banner had been erected between two large plane trees announcing the music festival. Cars were being directed to a field on the left. I parked alongside a black BMW. No VWs or Harleys in sight. In any case I was wearing a very ladylike calf length turquoise dress. Think Laura Ashley, without the print. A cacophony of beeps reverberated around the open space as dozens of dinner jackets, bow ties and shimmering evening dresses, pointed tiny black remotes to lock their cars.

I followed the human horde across the road to the entrance of the chateau and through a stone archway with rusting wrought iron gates held open by two giant urns overflowing with geraniums. A converted single story barn to the right had a sign Caisse over one doorway. Just inside were two more signs. Collect and Returns. The queue of people in the returns line was three times as long.

And so was born the moment that I decided to erm, lie. The returns queue was not moving. The collect queue was. I overheard someone give their phone number to the cashier followed by the date that they had reserved their tickets.

I reached the front quite quickly. I reeled off Deirdre's phone number and the date last Friday, without faltering. I was in the South of France and so there was none of the hushed tutting that accompanies slow moving lines in the UK. But I was still English enough to start feeling uncomfortable. The poor man confirmed that my reservation was indeed for one ticket? I nodded meekly. I could have been in line for the last kidney donation from the look on my face. I had reached the all or nothing stage and I could hardly back down now. He leaned across to his returns colleague who immediately sprang to life at her keyboard, alerting her queue. She nodded and motioned for me to move to the head of her queue. A manoeuvre I managed without making eye contact with anyone waiting for a return ticket. If you are already concocting my penance please bear in mind that I did only need one ticket and the queue was full of couples.

I paid with my credit card and walked as calmly as my conscience would allow, past both queues and towards the arena set out in a semi circle around the lake. In the centre of the lake was the stage. A canopied roof was strewn with hundreds of tiny white lights and was just beginning to illuminate as I found my seat...In the front row. Gulp.

The music was sublime. I spent the interval in my seat, examining the programme from cover to cover. The idea of wandering around with a glass of wine on my own was beyond my comfort zone. Even I have limits. Not to mention the fact that a particularly irate Frenchman with de in between his Christian and surname, denoting his affiliation with nobility, think double barrel surname in English if you want the equivalent, was glaring at me as he passed. He was seated at the back. He had been at the head of the returns queue.

The last ten minutes of the concert were the least enjoyable as I was facing the prospect of getting home (yep, it feels like home...) preferably with my car and me inside it. I didn't think pushing my R5 even downhill could ever be a good idea.

So, I looked at the map. I could go back the way I came on the D road. Yellow, narrow, twisting, on the map but direct or head across to the auto-route, miles, well kilometres, out of my way but at least if I did break down, through my own stupidity, at least help is at hand on the auto-route. I started the ignition and Beryl leaped into life. The fuel gauge however had much more of a problem. I watched and waited whilst the needle shuddered to a halt, nudging the red. Hmm. The car fairy had not been along and added a few litres. I now started to have real guilt pangs. I will run out of petrol because I lied to get a ticket. Simple. You can all forget any punishment, I was sweating like a proverbial pig.

I suddenly had visions of Deirdre wagging her finger at me through the rear view mirror. 'We left you in charge of Mother. How could you...'

Mother of course was being way more...hang on...irresponsible... says who? Neither she nor JL are married. She is not going to get pregnant and an orgasm twice a week is good for the heart and that is official. We had, at some point talked about sex and risks. I think it was the day Betty said she hadn't looked back since Jean-Louis had found her G spot. So after I finished smiling I continued that I had meant risks in the form of infections. Oh no dear. Nothing to worry about Jean-Louis always wears gloves when he is working.

It was one of the rare times when Betty really did not get what I was on about. If I mentioned Chlamydia I was pretty sure she would say. Yes, wonderful colours and oh, the perfume. I did not think you knew the names of exotic flowers Laura?

Allowing my mind to wander was great for calming my nerves but somehow I had to get back.

I took a deep breath, shoved a Meat Loaf cassette (it is still 1995) into the player. I was not expecting to go like a bat out of hell…just so long as I got back okay.

I took the direct route, freewheeling in neutral, a lot. By the time I got back to Les Collines the red light was blinking furiously. At one point, in the last five kilometres where the road is now like the back of my hand, I recalled an elderly French friend of mine, Marcelle, telling me about her trip to Ireland and how much she loved the laid back ways of the locals. She assured me that this was a true story.

She had been having trouble with her car and took it into a local garage in the village where she was staying in Cork. Betty would not have liked him, he didn't wear gloves. 'So what'll be the problem?' He had asked. Marcelle confessed to not knowing what any of the dials on the dashboard were for but felt that the one that kept flashing red must mean there was something wrong. He had nodded and asked.' Tis troubling you, so it is?' She agreed it was. He disappeared into his office. My friend took the opportunity to powder her nose. When she came back he proclaimed. 'It won't be bothering yer no more.'

She was amazed how quickly he had fixed it and started to reach for her handbag from the passenger seat. The garage owner waved his right hand. 'There'll be no charge. Have a good day now.' As he started to walk back into his office my friend peered in to her car. The engine was still running and sure enough she could not see the offending red light anymore. He had put a piece of masking tape over it...

****

It was pitch black in the driveway but the security light came on when I got to the edge of the fourth pine tree. In my relief to get back I had forgotten about our rule (mine and Betty's) about parking down the drive a little so that if the lights came on we would know it was not one of us. We had soon, after D and G left, found a way to circumnavigate the house without 'the Colditz effect' as Betty called it. Shines straight into my room. And believe me Laura at our age, she meant her and Jean-Louis', you don't always need a spotlight on the situation.

I walked round the back of the house and glanced up at the top floor. Ah, curtains closed. Betty was still out.

I had just put out my light, smoothing down my freshly laundered blue and yellow duvet, ready for dreams of who knows what, when the security light came on outside. Before I had time to sit up I recognised 'Merde' from Jean-Louis and a badly suppressed giggle from Betty.

They need not have worried as Betty's sling-backs did a far better job of alerting me to their arrival, clattering on each of the thirty two stone steps. However the next morning, being Monday, and nothing opened until lunchtime, I expected Jean-Louis had been invited for a sleep over, so I tried to exit the house quietly. I needed to get to the only petrol station that I knew opened for two hours on a Monday morning. It was too far to walk but was luckily downhill.

If you are still considering a penance, forget it. It duly arrived. I rolled back the roof on my trusted Beryl and stood for a moment, marvelling at the sound of silence, almost. The cicadas were now such a regular feature that you almost did not hear them.

I got into the car and turned the key. Wham, CRACK! I had never heard a car backfire before. I looked up at the third floor window for the next sound. 'Shit!' said Betty, clutching a fetching lilac negligee. Jean-Louis appeared behind her and gently waived.

I narrowed my eyes in frustration as Jean-Louis let one of his business cards float down from the landing window.

I had to decide. Laugh or cry. Betty solved the problem. "Coffee Laura?" she shouted.

I shrugged. "Why not."

As we all three met in the kitchen Jean-Louis announced "Your carburettor's fucked."

"English lessons coming along nicely I see." I stared at Betty.

Betty shrugged and Jean-Louis started to nibble on Betty's left ear. "For heaven's sake you two..."

ALL EXPENSES PAID

"Yes, stop it at once and go and get Laura some petrol. You can have your coffee when you get back."

"Just coffee...?"

"Shoooooo," Betty and I said in unison, flapping our hands towards the back door.

Jean-Louis looked down at his feet...

Saturday 26th August.

Take one Harley Davidson weekend, one Italian, one German and a body on the pavement.

It was nothing special but it was my favourite dress. A navy stretch cotton with a fine white stripe. It was sleeveless and fitted like a glove. In fact, once rolled up and in my suitcase could almost be mistaken for one. There was a small tear at the back just above the hem where I had caught it clambering over a fence last summer. I could not imagine a group of bikers caring about such details. They weren't all leather clad contenders for Monsieur Universe. There were lots of women in regulation jeans and tee shirts and children in studded waistcoats and bright bandannas.

I did not feel out of place, until now. I had been looking at all the stalls selling memorabilia. Native American Indian stuff and the usual Harley Davidson gadgets but suddenly I was tired.

I looked at my watch, it was eleven thirty. The group were due on stage at midnight. I had been there nearly six hours. I decided see what the band were like then I would head on back to the car, if I could find it.

Betty was away for the whole weekend so I could have the place to myself. I was toying with the options, tracing the outline of two sets of initials that had been carved into the pale wooden table top, watching a light breeze lift an empty polystyrene cup up and off the other end of the table, when one of the most intriguing, mischievous smiles caught my attention.

"Cigarette?" he offered, leaning across the wooden bench on one elbow, shaking loose a soft packet of Gauloise.

If only I could live on coffee and cigarettes, I thought.

I shook my head. Perhaps I would have to take up smoking or risk losing the chance of extending these brief encounters. Somehow I didn't think so.

I mean I had tried, but I had never quite got the hang of it. I could manage the flicked back wrist, cigarette balanced between the first two fingers bit, but the actual smoking seemed to upset serious nicotine addicts.

"Take it down!" they would cry. "Down where?" I would say. I managed to get the smoke to come down my nose once. I had to be prevented from doing dragon impersonations for the rest of the day. I did not like the taste and the smoke made me cough. I did however like the smell and this business of tapping the ash into the ashtray. It seemed to be lodged right up there with powder compacts, signifying being grown up and cool. Suddenly the eyes were joined by a taller friend who looked down at me with interest. They made a striking contrast. The 'eyes' answered to the name of Thierry and his friend was Zigo. Thierry was small, but perfectly formed, had wonderfully rich dark curly hair so often bestowed on the Italians and Zigo was taller, broader and had close cropped blonde hair underneath a red bandanna and was German. Thierry had eyes framed by the thickest longest lashes and a nose that wrinkled as he smiled. I was glad I had stayed. So there it was, that moment when refusing to take up smoking was about to change my destiny.

Zigo jumped as two girls approached them from behind, one poking him in the back. Thierry turned and smiled at the new arrivals. Oh well.

"Ciao!" said Zigo waving a hand at me as they turned and left. The two girls walked in front. Thierry looked back towards me but kept walking. He managed to indicate ten minutes by tapping his watch and holding up both hands. Yeah right I thought. What's he going to say to his girlfriend? He's got a headache. It was almost time for the stage to spring into life again so I downed my coffee and walked over in that general direction. Many of the stall holders were still doing business. I had bought some postcards earlier. A mixture of classic Harley Davidsons and Native American Indians. They all seemed to have such intensity in their expressions. I noticed there were still some young children around, but then the wet T-shirt competition had been on at six thirty, so chances were they had seen it all before. According to my programme, the band were listed as tres chaude. Very hot eh? I could hardly leave yet. I had my education to complete.

How come I was here? I could not decide. Was it because it was outside, the fact that no one would know me or just more of this 'feeling at home' scenario that had been getting stronger by the day. I tried to imagine myself in this situation back in the English countryside. But not for long as a voice chirped behind me.

"Ciao!" It was Thierry, he had returned and alone. Not much taller than me he literally breathed down my neck. "Oh." I said, turning round to see Zigo not far behind. "Hi."

No wonder my lottery numbers hadn't come up. I obviously did not know a safe bet when I saw one. "Where are your friends?" I asked meaning the girls of course. They both looked blank. So I tried. "Vos amies?" and looked around as if on a desert island and searching for any sign of life. "Ah. Gone." said Zigo solemnly followed by something in French to Thierry. He nodded, smiling at me in a rather 'desperate to convince me' kind of way. Our conversation was put hold as the next eight minutes were filled by an explosion of sound. Three Base guitars taking the lead, the group had the crowd jumping in no time. I was quite happy to stay but the boys (did I mention they were about twenty five) obviously had other ideas. After fifteen minutes, Thierry grabbed my hand and Zigo motioned getting a drink. At least we would be able to talk over by the bar. We sat back at the bench seat were we had first met, less than an hour earlier. Aah. our first anniversary, I thought . Zigo placed a small black coffee in front of me before sitting down with his pint and one for Thierry. It had only just occurred to me that he had not asked what I wanted. Thierry was sat beside me, grinning, tilting his head like an obedient puppy. I wondered if he had been home and changed, his dark blue trousers and crisp white shirt looked fresher than ever. He said something in French.

I shook my head. "Non?" he looked surprised. "Well, no not no. I mean, I didn't understand what you said."

Thierry looked at Zigo, who obviously was going to be invaluable.

"We go to a club. You come?" Thierry's eyes narrowed in concentration as Zigo spoke. They were probably about the same age but they looked so different. Zigo's skin was pale and taut over his young face. Thierry's face was more lived in, it moved with his emotions. "Okay." I heard myself say, mirroring their energy. Aah. NRG, my favourite radio station down here. Day or night it can lift any mood. (Now, it seemed, I was their advertising agency)

As we walked past my car I gave it a silent wave wondering if I would ever see it again, yet I didn't feel the least bit apprehensive. And then I had to make a choice. The black Golf GTI or the Peugeot 506. Sensible questions like. *Why aren't we all going in one car- Aren't we coming back here later- Am I being kidnapped?* were all far too difficult to construct in French and I did not think Zigo's English stretched that far. So, naturally with reliability in mind and a well respected rumour that I had heard, that you only live once, I chose the VW, which it turned out, was just as well.

Thierry examined and discarded three cassette tapes before plunging the chosen one into the machine. He turned to check my reaction as the music (an Italian love song, just as I had feared) filled the car from four speakers. At the same moment we were rudely interrupted by a loud beep from Zigo as he appeared through a cloud of dust having done a handbrake turn. "Tu aime?" he asked enthusiastically, ignoring Zigo who immediately sped off and out through the gates, onto the single file track that led down to the main road in the village.

"Mmmmm. I like it." I nodded, stretching my legs out in front of me, placing one foot on my handbag, out of habit. Seeing my thoughts elsewhere Thierry turned up the volume and sped off in chase of his friend. The silver 506 had come to a halt at the crossroads in the village, just by the phone box that I had used earlier. The sound of an approaching ambulance siren made me jump. Several people were gathered around a body on the pavement, opposite the phone box.

"Oh, someone's been run over." I said to Thierry who turned down the music. His dark eyebrows puckered in confusion. I walked my fingers along the dashboard, hopefully impersonating a character from a Lowry painting followed by an imaginary car and bang, collision. I was getting good at this. I'd had enough bloody practice with Eddy.

He shrugged his shoulders and raised his hands upwards. Obviously, I was not good enough. Zigo was leaning out of the window. Thierry wound down his and tilted his head. A conversation ensued. For once my excellent hearing was no use whatsoever. I was about to ask what Zigo had said when I noticed someone coming out of the bar carrying a pale blue blanket. They placed it over the body, all of the body. An ambulance came to an abrupt halt, as if surprised to reach its destination. The traffic started to move. I looked back at the scene to see a trickle of blood still seeping its way into the gutter...

"What happened?" I asked, feeling pretty sure that Thierry was holding out on me. His eyes darted from side to side, well his right eye, I could only see the one, as he searched for an easy way to explain the incident to this persistent English woman, who he wanted to please at all costs.

"No problem," he said at last. "Amicos..." he added taking his right hand off the steering wheel, clenching it into a fist and aiming the side of his hand into his chest. "A stabbing?" I gasped.

"Si, c'est ca." He looked pleased at our advanced communication. Well, that was reassuring. Here I was in a stranger's car hurtling off into the night, following another stranger, neither of whom spoke good English and I'd just witnessed my first friendly murder. In a vain attempt at some sort of control I asked Thierry where we were going? He told me. And the name of the town? He told me. The name of the club? He told me, nodding happily, interspersed with accompanying the chorus of the love song which I had a feeling was on a loop. It was about then that I added to my; 'If I were God list'. Share a common language. I mean keep your own by all means if it makes you happy, but let us at least be able to…then I remembered hadn't someone done that with Esperanto? Still what hope was there when as Valerie in Paris had pointed out when having a conversation between myself and an American au pair I thought you two spoke the same language?

Wot? I should cocoa.

Oh well I might as will sit back and enjoy the ride. Totally resigned and relaxed I was surprised to see Thierry tutting and pointing in front of us.

It was one of those times when you wished you had a video camera. Zigo was about hundred yards ahead of us now. We were out of the village and into one of those long straight tree lined country lanes that stretch endlessly before you. There was no street lighting only car headlights.

You could see that the camber of the road was pretty steep.

Thierry started to ease off the gas, giving his mad friend a little more space… for Zigo was half out of the car ... steering with his feet ? He was sat on the edge of the open window and leaning out, one hand on the roof of the car and the other waving at us. I say he was steering with his feet. I mean, how else?

Thierry tapped his head and then pointed at his friend. I nodded in amazement. Zigo's car seemed to be slowing down and beginning to veer towards the grass verge. But of course he was back in the driving seat in time to avoid a catastrophe.

'La voiture de maman,' says Thierry.

I nod again. The contrast is overwhelming. There I am being sedately wooed by some ageing Italian crooner and Mr Sensible with the cheeky smile and we are following his kamikaze German mate driving his mother's car.

Talking of mothers, Betty and I had left a message on the answer phone in case Deidre rang, letting her know that it was sooo hot we had headed for the hills and some fresher air.

Betty had been delighted when Jean-Louis said he was going to take a Saturday off in her honour. They had been invited to stay on a friend's yacht somewhere near Cassis. Wish you would come too, was Betty's parting shot. I had said something about two's company, three's a crowd. Was it a premonition? But hey compared to Paolo, Zigo could probably be a pussycat. My thoughts jumped back to the present as Thierry groaned. "Mais, non ..."

"What's the matter, er problem?" I corrected myself trying to remember to use words common to both languages. Thierry took both hands off the steering wheel and splayed them wide, palms upwards in disbelief.

"No Zigo," he announced.

And sure enough there was no sign of the car that had been ahead of us a few minutes ago.

"Aah," he sounded relieved as if remembering something. I was beginning to think I had been caught up in the making of a B movie.

"Regarde," shouted Thierry pointing up at his rear view mirror. I turned to look behind us and sure enough there was Zigo right on our tail with his lights out. I later learned that this was one of his favourite tricks, to zoom off into the distance, kill the lights; turn off the road somewhere, then come screaming up behind his unsuspecting friends in complete darkness. I thanked, whoever, for my choice of taxi. Almost immediately the Peugeot lights came on full beam as he swerved round us and back into the lead, lighting up the whole avenue of pine trees. Thierry and I gave each other a resigned smile.

"Is it far to the club?" I asked. He probably guessed what I had said by the last word. He held up one hand . Aah five minutes I presumed.

I heard it before I saw it. The sounds of music, laughter and general mayhem emanating from a night club full of people partying till they drop, or dawn, whichever came first. As we pulled up in yet another field-cum-car park, we saw Zigo emerging from his car, via the window, of course, as if being born... Zigo. A voice boomed from the gravel end, near the road. Zigo and his friend greeted each other with high fives, followed by a hug and slap on the back. Zigo with his athlete's body looked resplendent in his black leather trousers, cut away black T-shirt and red bandanna. His friend moved away as we caught up with him. I was not exactly sure what Thierry had just said but it seemed important that we stay together. Sure enough, one more shout of Zigo, only this time from the doorway to the club, did the trick. Zigo turned and beckoned. We walked casually but quickly past a long human snake of about fifty people and into the club. Thierry rubbed his thumb and forefinger together. Apparently Zigo's parents had loads of money. Once inside I decided to give my conscience about the inequalities of life, the night off.

The place was heaving, the sounds purely rhythmic. The Nightcrawlers fed our energy with *Push the feeling on.* The usual burgundy banquettes hugged the outer walls. Heavy glass topped tables were dotted in front with low padded stools placed either end. Latticework partitions provided shelf space for drinks. The dance floor in the centre was surrounded by mirrored pillars spaced at six foot intervals. Perfect if you were dancing alone but wanted to check out how you were doing at the same time. After all this was August in France, holiday time, so doing your own thing was nothing short of compulsory. I assumed Thierry had been here before but for some reason we had both been surveying the scene with fresh eyes. We both turned to each other at the same time and sighed. We both burst out laughing. We may not speak each other's language but we were on the same wave length. We were old friends already. From then on a happy sigh became our watchword. Thierry led me to the nearest seat and began motioning the bar and a drink. I pointed behind him. Zigo had appeared with a bottle of Vodka in one hand, a jug of chilled orange juice in the other and three tall glasses wedged under his right armpit.

The music was going through a frantic seventy's disco half hour, which meant everyone was generally throwing themselves about. I wanted to dance. I wanted a drink and I did not know what to do with my bag? This was not Essex. I could not put it on the floor and dance round it. Thierry saw my dilemma and lifted a pile of coats perched on the end of the seat to reveal four black handbags. Oh well, I thought, seeing as the whole evening seemed to be running on an over the limit risk factor. I said a quick prayer...*Dear God. Please look after my money, credit cards, mobile phone, car keys, house keys, English chewing gum and the photo of the man I love and can't have. Amen.*

Thierry leaped up onto and over one of the glass tables, as I downed my first glass of Vodka and orange. It was as though we were at a big private party; everyone seemed to know everyone including me apparently. My eyes followed Thierry and found him gyrating with a girl who had similar features to him, petite, short dark hair, extremely tanned with a definite Latin look. Zigo had disappeared from sight. I watched as a group of mainly twenty to thirty-somethings, moved to the music. I was without doubt the oldest there but the lighting was kind. Enough to see who you were dancing with, even if it was your own reflection, but not too bright to pick up any less than perfect features.

Thierry caught my eye so I went over and joined them.

It was one of those moments in life that you can savour forever.

I was more relaxed than I had been in weeks. I had not realised just how powerful Vodka and orange could be. And better still, at this very moment, no one, but no one knew where I was. Very liberating.

The main dance floor led out onto a patio of a similar size. Overhead a pergola adorned with an array of vine leaves reminded you were in Provence. A huge barbecue was still smouldering at the far end, near to another bar. No wonder it was not smoky in the club, the second thing I had noticed, with all this fresh air mingling between the two areas.

The first thing had been just how relaxed and confident they all seemed. There was none of that awkwardness and background tension that sizzles in some English clubs. I did not feel the need to stay with Thierry, I guessed we would find each other later...

The char-grill smell mingled with the sun-warmed fresh flowers. I had never been anywhere quite like this. A waft of some heady perfume moved past me as I found my way back to our seats.

The bottle of Vodka was now half full but there was still plenty of orange. I took my glass over to the bar and emptied a large scoop of ice into it. I could always sleep in the car tomorrow before I drove back I reasoned with myself as I topped up my glass.

Thierry was now dancing with a crowd; everyone was the centre of attention.

I looked up to see a girl towering over me. My eyes travelled up the long, long legs, clad unusually for this time of year in opaque high gloss tights. It was August. It was sultry. Her skirt was black and shiny and short. A fluorescent pink boob tube seemed to be restraining a resplendent bosom. By the time I reached the face, heavily made up including false eyelashes, the voice that came forth was more than a little agitated.

"What you looking at?" the face asked.

Good question I thought ...just what..? Then the penny dropped. I had walked in on the set of *La Cage aux Folles Three*. This young ladies' ample proportions had a familiar ring ... those of a man.

Wide-eyed by now, I quickly responded. "Oh, nothing at all, sorry."

She strutted off and had words with a man, the open shirt, hairy chest variety.

He was coming over to where I was still sitting.

I have a horrible suspicion, thinking back, that my bottom jaw was still in dropped position, really not helping the situation when 'he-man' said "You come with Zigo. German guy?"

He pointed him out. He was posing rather than dancing, checking out his reflection in one of the pillars.

"Well er, yes, no not really, more with Thierry the Italian guy." My hand shook as I gestured in his direction. He was back dancing with the girl he had been with earlier. She was standing on top of one of the tables hypnotising him with her belly button. The open shirt, raised his hand to smooth back his already immaculately gelled hair. Two heavy silver bracelets clunked together. I seemed to have stopped breathing.

"A warning," he says "Zigo likes women but he likes men best."

I now know how the proverbial rabbit in the headlights felt. I also seemed to have a coat hanger wedged in my mouth. I was speechless.

"Okay?" he countered, leaning over me.

"Okay." I squeaked . Anyway, I reasoned, I had come in Thierry's car, not Zigo's, so it would be no problem when it came time to leave. He would take me back to where I had left my car in a field…somewhere...surely. And then he was there, Zigo, all smiles.

"Zigo. Hi!" Before I could think of anything else to say he'd whisked away the empty Vodka bottle and jug and was heading for the bar.

Gosh, I wonder who drank all that then. I smiled to everyone in particular. Suddenly all the coats on the end of the seat bounced as Thierry landed at my side. I wondered if they all moved around like this during the week or maybe it was saved for the weekends.

But this was not just any weekend, it was August Bank Holiday weekend. Normally, in my recollection, which was not too reliable by now, anyway, normally Bank Holidays were a non event unless you liked getting stuck in coastal traffic jams as all the Brits suddenly remembered that they lived on an island. Ha! Everyone leaving either earlier or later than usual to avoid the traffic.

"Haaa." I grinned at Thierry, " Les Anglais..."

Having absolutely no idea why I was laughing he joined me.

"Les Anglais." He said raising his glass clinking it with mine.

I oopened my mouf to tell hom bout my warming, no, warning, silly girl. Gog this wodka is nice...

"Haa,haa..." I could not stop.

I could not see Zigo anywhere. Perhaps I had imagined the whole thing. Thierry was fanning himself with two drink mats.

"Hot?" he enquired

"Oh yesss." The word seemed to go on in front of me.

There was always going to be something magical about black VW's from now on. I was sure of it. Perhaps I should let their advertising people know just how much fun black VW GTI owners really have.

We had got past the kissing stage and had slid down the passenger seat. Our feet could go no further. My small navy and white dress had become a scarf. Thierry expertly ran his tongue around my left nipple. I had a fleeting, totally inappropriate, image of him as a baby. I stroked his head, running my fingers through his lovely hair. He lifted his head, letting his tongue travel the length of my neck, pecking me on the chin and then enveloping my mouth once more. I was wrong. We were not finished kissing yet. He raised himself up as he realised my squirming was due to his belt buckle sticking into my bare skin. The car park was totally still. Nothing moved. The throbbing beat from the club seemed far away and all was right with the world. A world which already had enough people in it I rationalised despite my blood alcohol ratio been unusually balanced. I had to ask.

"Have you got...?" Before I could finish my question, Thierry leaned across me and opened the glove compartment. Well. You know the scenes when someone wins the jackpot on the slot machines, it was just like that. Out they poured, square packets, oblong packets, blue ones, banana flavoured, ribbed ones, ones shaped like gold medallions, dozens of them. I was going to say we made love, well, okay we had sex, but it was lovely, all three times.

I think we might still have been there now if I had not suddenly remembered my handbag!

****

I lifted the pile of jackets to find my black handbag, complete with contents. It was four a.m. when Thierry pointed us towards the main door. There was no sign of Zigo.

Beryl, fortunately, stood out in the crowded car park. I waved at Thierry as he sauntered off in the opposite direction. Had this been one of the best nights of my life, I wondered? As I bent down to focus on the lock, the sound of "Ciao" made me drop my key. Zigo had been draped across the bonnet of my car. Odd place for a nap.

"My turn." He grins. Uh-oh. Have one, get one free seems to have got lost in translation. Even without the earlier warning I was not tempted to dance the light fandango with Zigo. But how to get out of it? I was not sure if being tired, mildly pissed and walking like John Wayne, would be sufficient reason as far as Zigo was concerned. I felt my 'best night' vibes begin to evaporate.

"Zigo, look, I'm not really..." I began.

"Zigo!" The voice came from the interior of a large black Volvo, two cars away. I could not see the owner of the voice but I was grateful. Zigo shrugged. Germans do it too? And off he went. Phew.

I was in no fit state to drive but I reasoned that the car park was private property. I would just move the car nearer the entrance for a quick getaway in the morning. Morning. Ha! Dawn was on the horizon as I reclined the passenger seat back as far as it would go and slid underneath my scratchy old travelling rug. I dozed and dreamed with a smile on my face. What a night...

ALL EXPENSES PAID

Wednesday 30th August.

French Kiss

It is only a twenty minute stroll down to the beach, well more of a cove really. Completely unspoilt with a few convenient flat topped rocks, perfect for spreading your towel and catching some rays but today I feel like the bustle of a beautiful town, so I jumped into Beryl and headed for Aix en Provence. The Cours Mirabeau is picture postcard perfect. *The gently spewing fountain at one end of taking of cameras had chatting of terrace it is alive but gently so. (*N.B. See what happens when you rely on Speech Recognition)

A very pleasant twenty six degrees and no discernable breeze, I scour the menus displayed in front of every restaurant and then remember that it is market day and head towards the brightly coloured, striped, canopied stalls. There's nothing I really want to buy, but browsing brings its own pleasures. Despite the beautiful weather the poster in front of the cinema catches my eye. *French Kiss* starring Kevin Kline and Meg Ryan. Could be as corny as hell or so bad it's good. Either way I am going to give it a try. Chances are the cinema won't be too full on such a lovely afternoon.

I emerged blinking into the late afternoon sunshine in time to get the last seat at Deux Garcons. The aperitif crowd filled the pavement seats. I got a table near the doorway. I placed my bag on the floor between my feet. I was just mulling over the scene in the film where Meg Ryan doses off in the foyer of a Paris hotel only to be startled awake and find her bag missing... This was unfortunate timing, as the waiter in his rush, caught the strap of my bag. He didn't fall but I reacted, no let's be honest, over reacted as the bag between my feet started to move. They say 'if looks can kill' well certainly my expression was homicidal. Poor man. Naturally he glared back.

Stay or go? I decided to stay. My French wasn't up to explaining my reaction. In any case he was too busy to care. I ordered a Pastis and it duly arrived with a small dish of black olives. I wondered how Betty was getting on today. Jean Louis was going round and she had hinted that they would like the place to themselves. He would supervise her swimming she assured me. I chuckled to myself as I thought about Deirdre and how she was so concerned and keeping the cover on the pool. If only she knew.

Betty would definitely love *French Kiss*, the film, I mean. Have to look out for it coming to Carry Le Rouet.

Thursday 31ˢᵗ August.

Travel broadens the smile.

My dear Jules,

A friend of Jean-Louis' has come round to fit a television in Betty's living room. Jean-Louis has custom made a satellite dish, disguised with the same colour as the render of the house. The centre of the dish with its microphone like protrusion was more of a problem. To leave it with its grey colour or try and disguise it...?

Of course all this is my fault. As you know, I brought my television and video over with me and since we watched programmes I had taped with Betty in mind, she realised how much she missed her favourites. Then she found out that with Sky, she could watch some of them. There's a lot of hammering and banging going on. I'm keeping out of the way.

So what else has happened? I finally went to St Remy en Provence. Voted best place in the whole of France to live. May even be in the western hemisphere. It is a microcosm of perfection. The tiny streets are decked with overflowing hanging baskets. Pavements and gutters washed down every morning. The clink, clink, of the local petanque team as they practice their skills. Each boule is polished carefully with the piece of cloth, dangling from pockets, in between throws. Every day is special. You feel as though nothing could ever go wrong here. Apart from a few postcards there is very little evidence of catering for the tourist. No tomato ketchup bottles on restaurant tables. No dubious translation of the plat du jour. My favourite being: Avocat et crevettes translated as Lawyer and prawns. For some reason avocat means, avocado AND lawyer but hey, thick *skinned, with a heart of stone..? Just saying.*

Then Betty talked me into going to a Gospel Choir concert in Alluch. It was fun but once is enough, if you know what I mean. Betty and beau went to a car show in Orgon. Apparently Betty is genuinely interested in cars, even new ones.

And you know I have been keeping a diary (you better keep these letters, they may become priceless one day ;-), well I decided to phone our favourite tabloid newspaper. I told them about my new life and that I've written an article called Travel Broadens the Smile. I thought they might be interested. I had a chat with the Features Editor. I was told that my article would not appeal to his readers as I sounded smug and Brits don't do smug. Pride comes before a fall and all that crap. I haven't quite decided yet but when I publish these articles in a book, I am going to phone the aforementioned supercilious bastard and say: Nah, na, nah nah.

Does that sound smug? Good!

Uh-oh. Got to go. I can hear Betty squealing with delight. I think it has something to do with the theme tune of Coronation Street, which I can hear. September tomorrow and the leaves have been turning brown and falling for ages. Autumn seems to be just around the corner.

Let me know if you can come over again before I leave (sad face).

Toodle oooooooo Lauwa. Xxx

Friday 1st September.

I'm being followed again. Axel?

No, beware the Minitel system.

Do it all the time don't we. Play safe. Just give him your phone number, do not tell him where you live, no problem. Only in France they have something called Minitel which allows anyone to find out, just from a phone number, the name and address that goes with it, or worse. You can see someone go into a house and then put that address into the system and bingo, the names of the occupants. But then this is academic in France as most people display their names by their front door bell.

Which is how I managed to be driving along with Betty one day, about a kilometre from the house, when a black VW came up behind us and started flashing its lights.

"Ooh, we're being followed," announced Betty gleefully.

She has been watching a lot of American movies since her daughter had been away.

Visions of Axel came flooding back, so I started to pull over. If necessary, Betty would protect me.

Betty insisted that I drive right to the end of the lay-by to give her time to check her lip liner.

"Hey, isn't that mine?" I queried with a side glance.

"No, it isn't. I bought one the other day after watching you use yours."

She was getting younger by the minute.

It was just five days since the Harley Davidson weekend, so I was not expecting my new Italian friend to show up, so soon.

I wound the window down.

The dark Italian curls nodded at Betty.

"Ciao...you have sister!"

Thierry suggested we all go for a pizza. Betty thought I should marry him. We chose our favourite toppings from the man in the pizza van, then we went back and sat in my car in the car park and watched as a middle aged, portly, balding man gets out of a black mini. He ducks down (making himself much more conspicuous) as he heads towards a white Mercedes. The black mini drives off with a much younger blonde female at the wheel who gives a wave in the general direction of the Merc. He flinches as he struggles to get the key in the lock.

We all three look at each other but true to form Betty announces. "Hope his aim was better earlier."

I nod with the enthusiasm. Thierry shakes his head slightly as if to check if it has come loose. But his frown asks the question. I am not sure I can explain it to him and start with.

"He had problem with key" I point at the key in the ignition. He nods. "The man and the girl in the mini..."

"Small black car," adds Betty.

"Hmm. Thanks. They were together earlier..."

I try to think of better ways to tell the story. Thierry is still looking puzzled.

"You try too hard Laura, let me."

"Man, key, car." Betty imitates the man's action with the key.

Thierry nods.

"Blonde woman, bed, man." Betty grabs an imaginary penis from her lap and starts waving it around.

It takes a moment before Thierry can decide how to react. His face says he gets the joke but his glance at me says, is she for real? I nod at his silent question.

"Capiche?" Betty practicing her Italian.

"Si, si," says a flusterted Thierry.

"So whya you no laugh?" Betty is in full mock mafia mode now. "Ok. I can see I'm just too much for your boy scout friend, so let's eat up then you can drop me home Laura."

I was hoping Thierry hadn't picked up on the boy scout jibe. I had told Betty about the assortment of condoms that Thierry kept in his glove box. Some things are better left unexplained.

****

We sat on the terrace with a coffee for me and a beer for Thierry. Just the one, he had to drive home. Pizza or no pizza he was so slim and the alcohol limit for driving is half that of the UK. We arranged that I would go over to his place in Cavaillon sometime next week, he would call me first. I asked if he lived alone? He hesitated far too long for my liking. Thierry had already told me he had a son but I got the impression he lived with the boy's mother, Thierry's girlfriend. I'm too young to be married he had wailed, the first time we met. I had to agree and in any case, there would be others after or even during me. He was still struggling to answer my question.

"Live with gatto." He finally said with pride. I shrugged. Did this sound like a girl's name? Betty was just emerging from the kitchen, carrying a bottle of water and a glass.

"He has a cat Laura. Maybe one..."

"Thanks Betty, enough with the music hall jokes. Goodnight. Bisous."

"Bisous," called Thierry.

He wanted me to meet his cat. Ah how sweet...

Saturday 2nd September

Blind Date with Jean Louis' younger brother.

Hi Jules,

Went on a blind date two nights ago, thanks to Betty.

Okay he was a lot younger than Jean-Louis, nearer my age but he still seemed ancient to me. He was passionate about his car, a brand new Alfa Romeo. Betty had just happened to mention my love of the old Spyders.

So there he was monsieur enthusiastic. Not much taller than me, say 5'6", slender, full head of wavy black hair and a ridiculous pencil thin moustache. A Spaniard in the south of France driving an Italian motor. Very European.

He'd chosen an Italian restaurant in Martigues, checked tablecloth, dripping candles stuffed into bottles, very 70's and he even made sure that they had my favourite dish on the menu, Osso Bucco. It was superb, light on the tomato and heavy on the lemon. Oh, you don't like eating veal. I forgot, sorry.

He owns a garage near Marseille. Yes, a successful business man and yes he wears gloves, so no nasty fingernails. He owns his own house, has two grown up sons who live in Spain and the UK, been divorced five years. Oh and he speaka de Engliss, albeit, like a character from a Spanish version of 'Allo 'Allo. Perfect you say? Wrong.

Naturally I still hanker after Thierry, who, after he turned up out of the blue last month, I haven't heard from him since. I know he's a concierge at a block of *flats not far from where we met; he's got a four year old son by his girlfriend who he sees once a week, the boy, not the girlfriend. He phones his mother in Italy twice a week and cries every time he puts the phone down, he told me. Perhaps he thinks I will be impressed by his sensitive side? Then again, Phillipe was fun.*

You're right, neither of them speak English

But Thierry and Phillipe know how to put Axel's condom waving into words and open a bottle of wine with one hand at the same time.

Anyway, poor old Jean-Louis' brother-what was his name-told me towards the end of the meal that he had a bottle of champagne on ice back at his place. So, I clutched my head and tried to look sad. So sorry, headache. That is universal for. Forget it...Not a chance... Isn't it?

More soon. Luv Laura. X

p.s. His name was Paolo.

Wednesday 6th September.

Thierry and the cat.

I followed the signs into Cavaillon. I went through three sets of traffic lights and then turned left. Thierry had been very good with his instructions, had drawn pictures when words failed him. There is usually parking available outside the apartment block where he was Guardian, he told me. I hoped he was right. Let me lose in any town with a one way system and I could be gone for hours. The green cross jutting out from the building on my right made me feel ridiculously happy. Ah the pharmacy; I was nearly there. As usual the green fluorescent sign flickered, pixilated and dissolved now showing the time and then the temperature. Thirty six degrees this afternoon with a chance of getting hot, humid and very sticky later. Well okay it didn't say all that, but you get my drift.

Thierry said he would try and be outside the building waiting for me when I arrived but to an Italian living in France, two thirty p.m. would just be a vague notion. I glanced past the pharmacy and saw an art deco facade with La Hortensia inscribed above the arched doorway. I slowed right down as I spotted a parking space directly outside Thierry's building. Unfortunately a dark blue car had just pulled ahead of the parking space ready to reverse into it. The sensible way to park, parallel to the curb. However the very idea of losing this space overwhelmed any sensibility. I drove into the spot head first, at an angle naturally. The blue car had started to reverse and then slammed on its brakes. There were two men in the car and both the driver and the passenger threw their arms up in the air. Tough titties, I thought. Then immediately wondered where on earth that saying comes from. I had to wait for the blue car to move away before I could reverse out, drive past the space and reverse back in, like a normal person. By the time I got out of the car Thierry was standing in the doorway with more than a bemused look on his face. He had obviously seen me arrive as he produced the necessary parking ticket and placed it on my windscreen. Two hours; that should do it. Thierry said something and seemed to be imitating the occupants of the blue car. And he was laughing. I am not sure the men in the car were.

I hadn't got a clue what he was saying but our communications skills were not paramount, so I forgot about it. The wonderful aroma of Italian coffee greeted me as Thierry unlocked the door to his apartment. It was pretty much as I had imagined, small, cosy, cramped, cluttered and masculine. There were photos dotted everywhere, presumably family rather than friends. One photo in particular in a silver frame was a miniature Thierry. The same copious lashes and the cheeky grin, no need for DNA tests with this one. No picture of the mother or at least, not that I could see. But Thierry's mother loomed large. Her photo, in pride of place, blue tacked to the fridge door. Where she dared to remind him, to eat well or not to snack? Motorbike magazines littered the coffee table. A bunch of dried mimosa dangled over the sofa with a rug thrown over. I probably wouldn't want to know what was underneath. Thierry lifted the old fashioned aluminium coffee pot off the hotplate and said, "Si?"

"Si." I agreed. As if I needed any caffeine to add to my adrenalin. My head was competing with other parts of my anatomy, debating whether our rendezvous was a good idea? Will we both be disappointed? Was the car an important element of the excitement? Only one way to find out. Thierry watched as I sipped at my coffee. The cat on hot bricks would be the perfect cliché. I put down my coffee cup and Thierry grabbed my hand. The bedroom was equally cluttered. Socks and CDs competed for floor space. A vase at the side of the bed with the single red rose, its head hanging made me briefly wonder who was here last. But not for long.

It turned out that the car was not a vital requirement after all. We were both dozing, equally sharing the duvet; funny how that can happen with afternoon sex but seems to become a battle during the night. In my grinning, sleepy state I raised my hand to my left ear. Arrête, I said. Seems a more powerful word than just saying stop. Although you see the word stop, all over France so why was I bothering? I had expressly told Thierry that tongues in ears, was a no, no. Either he didn't understand or he had forgotten. Because for me that tickling sensation in my left earlobe, was right up there with nails been dragged down a blackboard. Eek. I know some people love it but I hate it. Still not bothering to open my eyes I shifted on to my right side and said. "Stop it."

"Stop it?" Repeated Thierry from the end of the bed. My sense of direction is not my best feature but I knew Thierry's voice did not come from my left side. Thierry laughed and made clicking sounds with his tongue against the roof of his mouth. Fully awake now I rolled gently onto my left side only to be greeted by Thierry's Persian cat. I shot bolt upright and Thierry grabbed his cat, plonking her down on the floor.

"She like you." says Thierry grinning as he stands naked, hands on hips, in the doorway. He has returned with two glasses of wine. I only sip at mine. The alcohol limit in France is half that of the UK. And my limit is probably half of that again. I'm a cheap date.

Thierry drank half of his glass and placed it on the bedside table. He snuggled up to my left side and was just about to stick his tongue in my left ear when the song being played on the radio in the kitchen caught my attention. I had turned to playfully bite Thierry's tongue, before he could stick it in my ear. Unfortunately the song on the radio was one that brought back memories so strong, that I bit Thierry's tongue a lot harder than I had intended. He screamed and grabbed the side of his face. I was still listening to the lyrics of the Dina Carroll song. Thierry was looking at me in disbelief. He opened his mouth and blood trickled out. Oh my god what had I done?

Thierry leapt out of bed and went into the bathroom. I could hear him rinsing out his mouth. I felt awful. I could hardly explain about the song or maybe I should. I didn't want him thinking I was a closet vampire. For once I wasn't sure how to find the funny side of the situation. But I didn't have to wait long. Thierry returned to the bedroom brandishing a large chopping knife. "Now me." he says. Deadpan. He sees the terror in my eyes and allows me to suffer for a few seconds before rolling his eyes and going back into the kitchen. Phew.

He clambers back into bed pulling a face, as if he's been to the dentist. "I am *so* sorry." I told him. "Why you ...?" I can see Thierry searching for words. But we both knew what he wanted to say. I could only apologise again. I decided to blame the song. "Ah", he says, "Special song?" I nod and grimace.

It seems I am forgiven. Hopefully. We had just snuggled down when a sudden knock on Thierry's front door frightened the life out of me. Thierry however simply groaned, rolled onto his side and into his jeans that lay on the floor and yanked on a sweatshirt. He turned to grin at me and then glanced at the clock. It was five to four and time for me to get going. As Thierry answered the door, making sure I was out of view, I dashed into the bathroom. The usual blobs of shaving foam, uncapped after shave, wet towel on the floor and something resembling a science experiment in the base of the shower, hastened my decision to just get dressed.

Thierry walked me back to my car and he seemed a little anxious. He was looking up and down the street until he spotted a blue car. Ah the blue car. He

ALL EXPENSES PAID

seemed determined to explain the parking incident earlier. A police car went past and Thierry pointed. Bad parking, an offence in France? I couldn't think of anything more unlikely. I wrinkled my nose and shook my head. "Non, non." says Thierry. The parking place I had pinched had been unmarked police car. At least, I think that is what he said. Ah well, a blonde driving a UK plates car... what did they expect? One more nail in the coffin for the blonde stereotype.

Friday 22ⁿᵈ September

Once bitten...

Hey Jules,

Went into Martigues, my second home now and decided to try that Vietnamese restaurant, round the corner from the church, you remember? Well, there was a very nice waiter in there called Lok. I knew I was in trouble as soon as he shook his head at my pronunciation. He must have said it four times before I had to pretend to have a sneezing fit. It was just like that scene in French Kiss when Meg Ryan tries to say Luc. She was so sure she was saying it correctly.

Poor Lok, I just hope he didn't think it was anything to do with him. Ah well. Cute but too complicated. The food was delicious though. Pity it was closed when you came over. Don't you love it, I know, let's take our annual holiday, (nearly said vacation. Jeez, been watching too many movies, I mean films...agh!) at the height of the holiday season. Only in France.

You never said if all the photos turned out ok? Martin happy with his trip?

Anyhoo. Got to go.

Lotsa love,

L x

Wednesday 27th September.

"That's funny, Thierry didn't phone."

"Perhaps he's afraid he might get attacked again."

"Betty, he knows it was an accident."

"Ah yes, but once bitten..."

Even Betty couldn't manage to finish this one. She was shaking with laughter.

For all the years I had heard this expression, I never expected one day it would apply, literally.

"By the way, Laura."

"Yep Betty?"

"You got any more books by Janet what's-her-name?"

"Not yet, but I think it is the first of a series. What made you think...Oh I get it. Me and Thierry, sounds like one of Stephanie's predicaments?"

Betty nodded. She had her mouthful of olives. I had seen three green ones go in and no stones come out. Betty caught my 'nannying' look, as she called it. She gave an exaggerated swallow then opened her mouth.

"Stuffed!" She pronounced. "No stones, Laura. Will you quit worrying?"

Sure enough a large jar of pimento stuffed olives were on the kitchen table, behind her. But, *quit* worrying? Not a word Betty had used when I arrived.

Deirdre used to frown about her mother watching the commercial television stations, now she was becoming American -speak -friendly as well.

Betty grabbed one more large green olive from the jar, then replaced the lid. She threw the olive up in the air and caught in her mouth. " Reckon I could give that Grandma Mazur a run for her money."

"You most certainly could, Betty. You most certainly could."

Thursday 28th September

The one that got away.

Hey Jules,

I parked my car really badly the other day. (waits for comments...)

Now this is really hard to do in the South of France because no-one gives a shit; zebra crossings, one way streets, you name it, cars all over the shop. So, to get noticed I had to do something drastic. The reason behind all this effort? The local bobby...far too gorgeous to stay wrapped up in all that uniform much longer.

So I parked in a field, next to the village school. It was nearly going home time...this field was used as a cut through to the car park for the school. I would, very soon, be causing an obstruction. I hovered near my car...pondering my fate...'Now just come along with me madam...yes we will have to search you I'm afraid...have you got any weapons concealed about your person, etc etc..I've watched enough episodes of The Bill. I know how it all goes.

But then perhaps they don't get The Bill down here...Miserable git...okay very handsome git. I was still casually leaning against my car when suddenly a piercing whistle moved me into the upright position. I looked across to see him, gorgeous gendarme, with his hands firmly on his hips, whistle in his mouth and pointing at the open gate.

I jumped into my car straightaway, never mind the gendarme, thirty irate mothers were more than I could handle.

Cheers,

Lotsa Luv L. x

Sunday 1st October.

Countdown.

Deirdre and Gerard are due back in one week. I can't imagine how it will be. Me and the Betster have been having a fine old time. Deirdre had given me a contact number to call if I had any problems. I hadn't called and Deirdre hadn't phoned for the last three weeks. Betty spent the day with Jean-Louis and I did my chores. It didn't take long to mop all the floors and they were dry in no time. The study was the only room with wooden flooring. I was expressly forbidden to do anything in there, except breathe and answer the phone. Sunday evening had become movie night. So when Betty returned I told her I had a good one for us tonight: *Six Degrees of Separation*.

Tuesday 3rd October.

It had been a week since I had been expecting to hear from Thierry. I wasn't really worried. It wasn't that kind of relationship, but I hoped he was okay. I was making my ritual morning trip down the road when Thierry had appeared alongside the bread van. He gave me a lift back. I couldn't get into his car without smiling, giving an extra grin in the direction of the glove compartment.

As it turned out, he had the perfect alibi for not calling when he said he would. He was in hospital. No, not having his tongue sewn up, he'd got an ulcer and been told to cut down on the anti-pasto and the coffee. The hospital had suggested he try decaffeinated for a while. I think they may also have suggested he stopped breathing as well, for all the good it did.

He waved his arms about so much when telling me all this, I was afraid he might take flight.

We swam and laughed and marvelled at the weather.

Betty joined us at midday and offered to make lunch. Thierry said he had to cut down on pizza, well, mainly the cheese part so Betty made us a lovely spag bol. We told him, no parmesan. Thierry sulked but he did eat all his salad. We all drank Pelligrino with a dash of pomegranate juice. We could pass it off as Rose if anyone else should happen to pop by.

Betty kissed Thierry the customary three times with loud mwah, mwah sounds, before retreating for her siesta. He seemed to give Betty an extra hug. She winked at me as she went indoors.

****

As Thierry was leaving he explained that he would be having his bambino for the weekend and maybe the mother (his ex girlfriend, presumably) too. So this was goodbye. Ah well. We had fun and he really had forgiven me for the damage to his tongue. Although I am sure it gave him a slight lisp or maybe that was just my guilty conscious working overtime.

And then he produced a photo that I didn't remember being taken and handed it to me. As if I could ever forget Thierry with the cheeky smile. The photo was of the two of us by the barbecue at the rear of the night club. The horizontal white lines on my navy dress are skew whiff and I have the most ridiculous smug expression on my face...

Saturday 7th October.

Betty appears for breakfast wearing a black armband over her embroidery analgise housecoat.
She manages to keep a very straight face while I say to myself, who, what, how, where, when?
I'm thinking anniversary of something personal? I tell her sit down and tell me about if she wants to...
By the time I take her breakfast tray into the living room she is wearing it around her forehead.
"You sod." I said, grinning from ear to ear.
"Yes, ze enfants terrible is arriving very soon."

Knew those episodes of the *Golden Girls* and *Allo Allo* would go down well but I didn't think she would be so good at impersonating the characters.

****

I went to Avignon market as soon as I realised there was a book fair on as well. Books, magazines, postcards. I especially love the postcards, when I can read the writing. Little snapshots of history. But the old magazines soon caught my attention. They were so big compared to their modern counterparts.

I bought a copy of *Paris Match* August 1954. I was a one year old when Colette was having a State funeral. When time travel is available through Thomas Cook

I am going to straight back to have a chat with the woman who has influenced my life, more than any other...so far.

Sunday 8th October

Back to Normality

Jean-Louis came round last night. We had a, re-covering the pool, ceremony. Betty has put her fun clock back in her pad. I have cleaned the whole place, even the skirting boards. Double checked for stray chocolate truffle wrappers, (strictly forbidden). Wiped the cassette tape in the answering machine, (Jean-Louis's idea). Bought twelve jars of apricot jam and steamed the labels off. Replaced with handwritten ones by Betty.

Deirdre rang to tell us not to wait up. They wouldn't be back until *after* Mother's bedtime. Unfortunately I had put Deirdre on speaker phone.

"Laura, what's that strange noise? Is everything all right?"

"Yes, everything is fine. It's just...just..."

Betty was prancing around the room holding a quoit over head, halo style. After a very loud snort of laughter she frantically pointed to the radio.

"The radio, Deirdre. Yes, it suddenly went off station. Quite windy here."

I immediately turned my back on Betty as I knew what was coming next.

"Is Mother there?"

"She is. Do you want a word? I was just making her some Ovaltine."

Betty had now picked up my bottle of Jack Daniels. It was on the bottom stair, I was taking it back up to my room when the phone rang. Betty looked at me and tipped her head to one side, glancing at the bottle, mouthing, Ovaltine?

"No, no. Tell her we will see her tomorrow. Goodnight."

And with that she was gone.

"Betty..?"

"I know Laura. It sounded like my daughter but..."

"She didn't say, silly me, once. And she stuck to the point."

"Spooky."

"Perhaps Gerard has had her cloned?"

"Yes Betty, of course, why didn't I think of that."

Monday 9th October.

Somehow I have agreed to go to a dance class with Betty.

"Betty, I have two left feet."

"You mean your dancing is as bad as your singing?"

"Yep, that really is encouraging..."

"For goodness sake. It's fun, it's exercise. You can't sit and read all the time."

"Ok. I know. Just for you."

I had a sudden thought. "It's not a set up is it? No passing cousin on Jean-Louis' side?"

"Such a suspicious mind, young Laura. No good will come of it!"

"You've been at the Bette Davis films again haven't you?"

"Moi?"

One of the best things about meeting Betty was being able to enjoy our shared passion for old movies. And we both agreed, they were best watched on a Sunday afternoon, in front of a blazing log fire, only pausing to toast more crumpets and trying not to burn yourself with the long handled forks. Thirty two degrees, cicadas in the background and blazing sunshine just didn't work. But it didn't stop us trying to remember and quote lines from our favourites films.

Thursday 12th October.

"That Ian McShane reminds me of your Thierry. Same hair."

"Yes I suppose he could be a much older brother."

"Nearer your age in fact."

"Funny isn't it how some women prefer younger men."

"Okay point taken."

"Are you ever going to..?" I stopped. I had tried broaching the subject before to no avail. Betty was adamant; her love life was nothing whatsoever to do with her daughter. I think Betty's philosophy of live for today was constantly overshadowed by her fear of rejection. She hadn't voiced it exactly that she was sure her relationship with Jean- Louis couldn't last much longer. And she didn't need any 'told you so' lectures or worse, overwhelming sympathy from her daughter. So her way was the best way.

"It is a lovely area."

"Sorry Betty, where?"

"Where they filmed the series. Hang on, is it Suffolk or Norfolk? Lavenham, isn't that where it is?"

"Sounds about right. All tranquil, flat and afternoon teas."

"Very tweed skirts and spinsters."

"Green Wellies and walking the dog."

"Afternoon vicar- lovely day for it."

"Barbours and Volvos."

" Horse and Hound. Country Living. Harpers and Queen."

"Cucumber sandwiches. China tea."

" Dented, red tiled hall floor, walking sticks in the stand."

"Constable country."

"Bicycle with shopping basket on the front."

"Green tomato chutney."

"Best Blooming dahlia competition."

"Henry and Henrietta."

We hadn't noticed Deirdre standing in the doorway until she added "Twin set and pearls."

Betty and I looked at Deirdre and nodded.

ALL EXPENSES PAID

"Homesick mother?"

"Good grief, for that lot? No darling. We've just been watching Lovejoy and found ourselves hurtling into at a cliché competition."

"Lovejoy?" Repeats Deirdre

"You know Ian McShane. That wheeling dealing antique dealer. Gift of the gab. Ladies fall at his feet."

Not sure why Betty bothered, she knew Deirdre wouldn't know who we were talking about. But she had asked.

"I'm not homesick either." I added wistfully. Deirdre sensibly decided to ignore my comment. We still had an open plan about me finishing at Xmas. Now that Betty had been here over twelve months in the South of France, she benefitted from the climate and the lifestyle in general, and my help I knew, was quite superfluous. I would have to leave before Christmas. And if the time came that Betty needed more help, meals on wheels, the equivalent being three courses with wine would be delivered each day. Plus the care allowance would be provided and any nursing through Deirdre's Mutuelle health insurance. Whichever way I looked at it, I was history.

Saturday 14th October.

Madonna who?

"I told my dear darling daughter that we were going to watch Madonna on M6, pronounced, cease and she said..."

"I can imagine. What's M cease?"

"That wouldn't have been so bad. No, she said Madonna who?"

"Crikey."

"How did she get so old?" Betty looked up at me. She was sitting in the middle of her two-seater sofa. Knittting, to her left and a book to her right entitled *The Celestine Prophecy*. "Deirdre says it's very good but badly written...whatever that means."

"Don't look at me; I get enough flack from Julia about my grammar. I told her I was away the day we did that. Turns out I needn't have lied. None of us were taught the stuff, so we just tell it like it is. Lump it or like it."

"Pick a pew, it starts in ten minutes."

I dragged the leather poof across the floor and positioned it so that I could sit with my back to the edge of the sofa.

"Brought that back from Morocco. Last holiday I had with Marietta. Everyone thought we were mad. It was such a foreign country back then." Betty stopped and surveyed my doubtful look. "We brought back the skin, *then* stuffed it!"

"Ah, thought it would have been a bit heavy. Having a blonde moment. Talking of which..." I grabbed the remote and un-muted the sound. Smoke and glitter balls filled the screen. Betty swung her legs upon to the sofa. We were set.

"Have we pre-ordered interval drinks?"

"We have. Special delivery."

I had only been joking. "What have...?"

"Shoosh. Here we go."

Deirdre was out for the evening and Gerard had his Do Not Disturb sign hanging off the doorknob, to his study.
He had a paper to finish by Monday morning and would most probably be working and wearing headphones, listening to Mahler, the current favourite. Gerard's study was the only room in the house without natural light. I could never work in a windowless room but he said it helped him focus. It also helped the unseen arrival of our interval drinks.
As the word PUB scrawled across the screen there was a gentle tap on Betty's outer door.
No prizes for guessing. Jean-Louis. But what I hadn't guessed was the tray bearing three salt rimmed glasses and a jug of margarita over crushed ice. Party time.
Jean-Louis stayed for the rest of the show and snuck out just after eleven. Pushing it really, as Deirdre could be back at any moment.
I had conveniently popped to the loo, as the show ended to give the love birds some smootchy time.
They were adorable and cringe worthy, all at the same time.
"Jean-Louis wants me to get one of those conical bras." Said Betty, pan faced.

"Sure he does Betty."

"Actually what he said was. You want comical bra, I buy you comical bra."

"You've slipped into Marx Brothers mode again haven't you!"

"You know me sooo well. Now go and get some beauty sleep."

I pecked Betty on the cheek and went downstairs to my room. I was just in time to hear Deirdre come in and Gerard's study door fly open. They met on the staircase. I couldn't see them but I could hear them. Betty had not been exaggerating. They were like a couple of teenagers. You'd think Deirdre had been away for days instead of just the evening. Now, what to do? I could read and plug my ears or put my walkman and headphones on. I chose the latter and I could still hear them through the walls. Forty minutes later I heard the bathroom door open and close. Phew, at least I could go to sleep now. Seconds were usually kept for Sunday mornings.

Sunday 15th October

Hey Julia,

It's me, but then you probably knew that from the postmark and the stamp and the airmail sticker and my writing ;-)

How you doing, me old fruit bat? Time is flying here. Got to decide about finishing soon. Boo hoo.

Dropped Betty off by the church in Le Carry this morning. All in her Sunday best. I'd shoved a holdall in the boot, with a change of clothes. She was being picked up by lover boy to go...wait for it...go-karting! She promises if Deirdre

ALL EXPENSES PAID

ever finds out she will swear I knew nothing about it. Gotta love her. Betty I mean.

Keep hearing that Michael Jackson song. You are not alone. It really haunts me. I'm not sure I even like it but it just seems so sad.

Anyway, D is off to Brussels on Tuesday until Friday so that'll be good, as long as we ignore Gerard behaving like a puppy, who has been abandoned his mistress.

More soon.   Take care.

L xx

Friday 20th October.

Will the real Gerard please stand up?

Hi Julia,

Just a quick one. Hope you're okay. Sad you can't come over again but glad you love your new job. And yes, Christmas adverts, I realise you have to get people signed up. Absolutely no mention of the C word here and shops don't start selling stuff until the first week of December. Quite right too.

So, news. Well. D is back from her few days in sproutland and it is her birthday tomorrow. All very low key, apparently. Betty has organised a cake for teatime and then D and G are going out for dinner somewhere, just the two of them.

And yes, as you suggested, I have been looking in the paper every day for jobs down here but there is nothing I can really do, apart from bar work, which I would hate. So it seems I will be back before you know it.

Au revoir,

Xxx Laura xxX

Sunday 22nd October.

Gerard flounces into the kitchen and announces that he needs space. Of course when it was just me and the Betster we cooked in the kitchen, whatever, whenever. Betty has a small hot plate and a microwave in her place, ok for the odd drink or soup but no good for main meals. I am well aware that this dynamic, of the four of us is very different. To say Deirdre wears the trousers is an understatement. Still can't quite get my head around *this* Gerard; so different to the one that interviewed me in Brixton. That seems to be the thing about couples. Some call it compromise, give and take. I call it selling out. When I find someone who is happy for me to be ...me... Dream on, is always Julia's comment.

"Sorry Gerard, you were saying?"

"I need my kitchen. To myself."

Before I can ask him to clarify, he has flounced back out of the kitchen and I can hear him going upstairs. Not good. The divide between me and Betty and Deirdre and Gerard is getting uncomfortable. You can expect a certain amount of, what do they call it when you start to identify and even come to love your kidnappers? I don't think I will run that one past Betty. She would laugh but would also be tempted to repeat it. Deirdre would not think it funny.

I was in the kitchen dividing up the remains of D's birthday gateau, into four, when I heard the whoosh of expelled air that comes from Gerard's mouth when he is not 'appy. Before I could turn round, he was gone.

It was five o clock. Time for tea. Betty was making a brew upstairs. I had developed a penchant for Lapsang Suchong with lemon. So refreshing in the heat. It was still getting up to thirty degrees by mid afternoon but now as the sun started to slide behind the hills, the temperature was dropping sharply. Soon be time to go back to earl grey and shortbread. A fresh supply had arrived yesterday, courtesy of Audrey.

"Has Audrey ever been out to visit?"

I asked Betty as she poured the tea using the silver strainer. I only had to see a tea strainer and I was catapulted back to my long three weeks with Lady Belcher.

"Penny for them?" It was ages since anyone had said this to me. My grandmother used to, whenever I 'drifted off', which was often. I had told Betty all about my first live-in care assignment, no need to repeat that, but I did think I should bring up about the atmosphere between us all.

"I was just...oh, yes, Audrey. Has she been over?"

"No. She says her travelling days are over but if someone were to go and fetch her and bring her...Laura!"

I had gone again. Poor Betty, I was being lousy company. "Here, take your tea and I shall eat both pieces of cake if you don't tell me what is wrong."

Betty knew my Achilles' heel. I heard cake, chocolate too. I focused.

"Sorry Betty. It's different now isn't it?"

"Bound to be Laura. I think we need to have a pow-wow, don't you, all four of us. We are all tiptoeing around each other. It is driving me crazy too. I'll have a word with D this evening. Remember there is always an answer, even if it is no."

"Okay, sounds good." I said through mouthfuls of wonderfully gooey chocolate ganache. I licked my pastry fork and grinned at Betty.

"How about I make myself scarce this evening so you can chat with D first?"

"No, Laura, that's exactly what I don't want. You live here too, for the moment. We will discuss it together. So don't go out, or the moment will be lost."

ALL EXPENSES PAID

I was still in favour of the tiptoe approach. But what do I know?
Deidre was out at a 'Get to know your inner child' meeting, all day. It was almost nine pm, when she got home and Gerard was having a giant sulk in his study. You always knew. He huffed, puffed and sighed until someone asked if he was all right?
Betty, wisely, abandoned the plan, to have a word.
I went up to use Betty's corner bath whilst she was having a drink downstairs. The mornings were easy as both Deirdre and Gerard left for work at seven thirty. I could use the bathroom after that, no problem but the evenings were more difficult to gauge and Betty knew I liked a nice long soak, every now and then, hence I used her place. Deirdre had suggested Betty had a large walk in shower. Much easier Mother. Betty told me, she means, if I have another stroke. I could see both sides of this argument. I am glad Betty won. I slipped down under the bubbles, the scent of patchouli tickling my nostrils and sighed. Not attention seeking, Gerard version, just my own, relaxing into the moment, kind of sigh. Happy to be here. Note to self: Think no further.
I was okay until I got into bed, then my head started to buzz. The 'what if' brigade had taken over my thought processes. Damn. I told myself to shut up and go to sleep. We would all talk it through tomorrow. End of. I smiled to myself as I realised I had picked up this expression from an American film I had seen recently. So now, I was wide awake, trying to remember, who said it and which film...?

Monday 23rd October.

Louise saves the day.

There is a definite nip in the air this morning. I closed the French windows against the breeze. It was only seven am and I didn't normally venture downstairs before the workers left but I really needed a hot drink. Alert the media. Laura has raging sore throat.
Betty offers lemon honey and whiskey. Deirdre offers a book. Gerard thinks I should take antibiotics. (So French)
I make a large mug of lemon and honey (omitting the whiskey for now) and curled up in my cosy armchair, in my room. Deirdre has left the book she mentioned propped up against my door.
How to Heal your Life by Louise L Hay. Hmm. How on earth is a book going to ease the feeling of razor blades doing a juggling act in my throat? Even swallowing the soothing drink was painful.
As I start to flick through the book a handwritten note falls out.
Laura. How about we have a chat this evening, all four of us. Things have become a little strained and we need to sort it out. Nothing that can't be solved. After supper. 8.30ish? Love D. X
P.S. Have a look at what Louise has to say about throat problems. ☺
Now whereas Betty was all into exercise, with her yoga and dancing, Deirdre was more interested in the cerebral and the metaphysical. She craved the calm that meditation brought...she said. She had started a new course through the University in Marseille where she was doing her PhD. Betty had already told me that the house had been Feng Shui-ed a few months back, until Gerard

complained that he couldn't find anything. So I really wasn't expecting too much. The thought and the gesture however were really appreciated. At times like this I wondered if Deirdre would manage to produce the grandchild that Betty so obviously wanted and what sort of mother she would make. Then I remembered soon after I had arrived, Betty had shown me the spare filing cabinet in their study. Betty had pulled out the first drawer. The first file was labelled, first child, name, DOB, weight, eye, hair colour. The second file read: First child. Nursery school, interests, known allergens, play dates.

The sixth file was labelled University. Betty watched my incredulous expression become fixed. I had even stopped blinking. She nudged me. I shook my head, to bring myself back into the real world. At least they didn't have dates on them that would have been really tempting fate. Betty had smiled in her-it's not just me then- way, when she is talking about her daughter. She asked me what I thought the second drawer held? She gave a nod and sigh when I suggested, second child?

She is such a planner. So organised and with her work and her studies it's invaluable but...Betty stopped there. I knew what she meant. And Gerard, how would he fit into this master plan? I really couldn't see him being the modern man, changing nappies etc. But I am told it is an experience that changes everyone. Way too scary for me. What if I don't like the changes? I was reaching that now or never period (pun intended) of my life. I could barely manage to look after and keep alive, the plant Julia gave me last Christmas, so I didn't think I was equipped to actually 'own' another human being. Nope, I'm pretty sure, I'll just settle for looking after other people's...people.

With my future firmly sorted I opened Louise Hay's book towards the back and scanned a list of illnesses. Yep, yep, yep. Got them all. This is why I stopped looking at medical books some years ago. I find them absolutely fascinating but I sometimes wonder if we can know too much or is it a case of a little knowledge is a dangerous thing. Hmm. Throat problems. Maybe Deirdre was on to something here. For once I was nodding as I read but in a good way. Storing emotion in our throat. I could relate to that. Keeping emotions bottled up, instead of letting them out. Not saying what you really feel. Now I could see where this was going. Clever. And I thought Deirdre was only an expert on dead humans.

As a child I had recognised those first tingles in your throat, when you start to get upset about something. That lump in your throat, certainly wasn't imagined. I tried to think back to how many times that feeling had become trapped, producing tonsillitis, over and over again. This all made sense but what was the solution? You couldn't go through life, not feeling anything. As I thought this, there was Miss Belcher again. Amazing I hadn't had a sore throat whilst I was there. But maybe the fact that I had spoken about her, had got it off my, erm, throat, had done the trick.

ALL EXPENSES PAID

Wed 25th Oct

Hi Julia,

Just a quick note. Deirdre has lent me this brilliant book. You have to get a copy. It's called **You can heal your life by Louise L Hay**. You know how I'm always getting sore throats, well, I had a corker two days ago and now it's gone. The pain, not my throat. Have a look and see what she says. You know the old expression about getting it off your chest, well, it's a bit like that. Not bottling things up and once you have realised the underlying emotional aspect of what ails you, you can start being more positive to prevent it reoccurring.

I'd been quite down since D and G got back, with the thought of leaving and all that. Plus getting frustrated, having to tiptoe round the house, literally, they go to bed so early. Anyway, we all had a good chat and have agreed about times to use the kitchen and bathroom. D's okay really but G is so obsessive, if you move anything in the bathroom two inches to the right...

So, talking it all through, we have managed, I think, to be a bit more tolerant of each other's foibles.

Well, theirs', because as you know I don't have any!

All for now. Hope you and hubby are ok.

Love Lauraxxx

P.S. Let me know when you get the book and what you think.

Wednesday 1st November.

Deadlines.

Someone has left a copy of today's *Daily Mail* on the seat. I glance around the cafe expecting some irate traveller to pounce on it. It is mid afternoon so it must have arrived with someone on a morning flight. Well done Sherlock. My powers of deduction have been sharpened with great weather, food, wine and company. Because I have to admit I never expected my charge to be so much fun. Thank goodness old Ma Belcher didn't put me off this caring malarkey for good.

I had to make a plan. Christmas was the deadline and I still needed to work and it was becoming more and more difficult to adjust to having Gerard and Deirdre back full time. I would ring the agency back in England just as soon as I had given my notice. I would tell Betty first, then Deirdre.

I looked round and no-one was charging toward me, hand outstretched, demanding I hand back their paper, so I laid it on top of the table but away from me so that I could be forgiven for thinking it had been left for all and sundry to read. It had only taken me seconds to flick through it. The news was either depressing or downright 'who cares?' gossip. The weather in London was awful. I was dreading going back.

I should take French lessons. Genius. It has taken me four months to come up with this idea. I knew a few more words but as to stringing a complete sentence together...In any case, I reasoned, there are so few jobs, why bother. The Mail had four *pages* of jobs. Le Figaro had four jobs. So many of the jobs in this region were also seasonal. How did people manage in the winter? Nope, I had to stay realistic.

I ordered a chocolat chaud. It was just the right temperature for drinking or as my British chums would say. 'Not very hot is it?'

Wednesday 15th November.

Dear Jules,

Well, I've done it. Given my notice. Leave on 17th December. Boo-hoo. Just to add insult to injury, all the cafes seem to be playing, Still haven't found what I am looking for.

Did you see the GP on Sunday? Mika Hakkinen in a coma! I watched it with Betty. Thank goodness he came out of it the next day. Betty was all for sending flowers to the hospital. Bless her. Had a fab haircut on Tuesday. A bob, what else? Saw a beautiful gold, shimmery, mac for 899 Francs, in that shop we went into in Martigues, next to that haberdashery shop that looked as though it had been preserved in the nineteen fifties. Ok, the mac was £90 and probably not shower-proof but so practical in the middle of winter in England. Ha!

I'm reading the Alchemist by Paul Cohelo at the moment. Tis good. Thought provoking stuff.

Catch you later. XxX LauraXxX p.s. No I didn't buy the mac.

Thursday 16th November.

"Roll up, roll up. Tickets for the circus tonight!"

Betty was standing in my bedroom doorway. It was eight fifteen a.m.

I heaved myself up onto my elbows. I glanced at the clock.

"Whoah, sorry Betty, slept through my alarm. And I didn't hear (I pointed to the next room) leave this morning."

"Nah. They went early. And JL has already been and gone"

"Blimey, that was a quickie."

"Says it sets him up for the day."

"I was only..."

"Yep, me too. He just dropped these off." Betty waves three tickets at me.

"The circus...really?"

"What, you too old for the circus? I know you hate pantomimes, so..."

"Well, I've only ever been once."

"It's suitable for vegetarians..."
"Deirdre's going?"
"No, sweetpea. That was a joke...You ok?"

"Yeah. Sweetpea. You haven't called me that before."
"Sorry, didn't mean it to sound patronizing, it's just..."

"Oh, no you didn't, it wasn't, it's just that's what Julia calls me, because I fall over easily."

"And I'm the one who needs the cane! You've got that look again. Stop it, or you'll get me going. Look the circus is animal free, is what I meant. Just high wire acts, clowns and stuff. Come on, it'll be a laugh."

Sunday 19ᵗʰ November

There can *be* only one.

"I'm not sure this is really my kind of..." Betty stopped mid sentence as I suspected she would. "Oh now I see."

We were watching the opening sequence to Highlander with Adrian Paul. The little glimpses of history, fascinating, and the sword fighting, athletic, energetic even balletic at times but in my mind the whole series was about following Duncan MacLeod's every move. Every muscle flexed, every bead of sweat, each eyebrow raised.

"I don't remember seeing this before. Or should I say him, before."

"Well I don't suppose it's a genre that would normally appeal. Let's face it on paper..."

"Oh yes but the reality." Betty fakes a swoon. "And that's why you have that ridiculously long Mac. Do you think if you imitate him enough, he will appear?"

"I doubt it but I do have his photo in my purse so that if I get run over by a bus, I'm hoping the paramedics will send for him, thinking he is my next of kin..."

"Ye gods and little fishes. What will you come out with next, Laura?"

There was a gentle tap on Betty's door. Neither of us had heard anybody coming up the outside staircase. It must be Deirdre. As big as she was, she still managed to be a light footed.

And she often wore trainers that on dry stone steps were inaudible. Betty hit the pause button as Duncan was in mid, cape-flowing, sword fighting mode. "Entree" called Betty.

Deirdre poked her head around the door. "We're just off to the Geant. Either of you want anything?" Deidre glanced at the screen and back at me and frowned. It was a complete role reversal. Deirdre was the mother and Betty was the child, with me as the disruptive babysitter. Deirdre's face said, what on earth are you watching?

Betty as usual could not resist making the situation worse. "You've got Gerard, now run along while we enjoy ours."

"Um, so nothing then, for either of you?"

"No thanks." We said in unison.

"Oh okay then. Well..." Deirdre stopped. We could see the cogs whirring. We knew she was sifting through the usual choices. Don't stop up too late mother. Are you sure this won't give you nightmares? And have you thought about Christmas? Betty and I waited patiently and gave Deirdre time to process her thoughts. She finally shrugged, said nothing and gave us the merest nod as she closed the door.

I hit the pause button again and Betty hit the volume control. Oh dear. The soundtrack that accompanies the fighting scenes in Highlander is not exactly subtle. And Deirdre would still be in earshot as the heavy metal band boomed from Betty's sitting room.

I would be lucky to last until next month at this rate. "Stop winding her up Betty, you are cruel."

"Yes Miss, sorry Miss. It was an accident. I really meant to turn it down but in my excitement I got the control the wrong way round."

"Okay forgiven. Want to finish watching it?"

"Is the Pope Catholic?"

Of course I had seen them all, every episode, and more than once. Betty commented on what a perfect couple Duncan and Tessa made. Ah yes, too perfect to be allowed to continue in the world of a television series. But of course I wasn't going to spoil any of it for Betty; she should be allowed to enjoy the series just as I had. Except that, I had only brought two episodes with me. I could sense another trip to Fnac coming on.

We had just started watching the programme again when the phone rang downstairs. Neither of us took any notice as we knew the answer phone would pick up any messages and they would probably be for Deirdre and Gerard anyway. And then we heard the clatter of footsteps outside. This time it was Gerard for sure. "Laura, there is phone call for you. It is your friend Julia."

"Okay Gerard, coming." I looked at Betty as she hit the pause button. "No you carry on. Remember, I have seen these before. Wonder what Julia wants. Hope she's OK"

When I got back upstairs Betty had discovered the slow motion, frame by frame, button on the remote control. "I can't decide which look, I like the best"

She had obviously completely forgotten I had been downstairs to take a call from Julia. I wonder how Adrian Paul would feel to know his latest adoring fan is 82 years old.

"I know what you mean. I still can't decide and I've watched them over and over."

"How was Julia, everything OK?"

"Yes she was just ringing to tell us we have to watch television tomorrow evening. Apparently Princess Diana is going to be interviewed, mainly about her marriage."

"Can't see that going down very well with the powers that be."

"Probably not, but she does seem capable of speaking her mind more than most."

Sunday 10th December .

Leaving Gracefully.

"Perfect timing," Betty exclaimed on the Sunday morning, just one week before I was due to leave.

Deirdre looked up from reading her latest crime thriller, carefully replacing the book mark before closing the book. She never, ever, laid an open book face down. It damages the spine. She had tried telling her mother but she just wouldn't listen.

Where does she get all her ideas from? Betty had marvelled to me one day. You are so different. I agreed. More like her father perhaps? I ventured, but as usual Betty would not be drawn.

"What is, mother?" Deirdre gave her mother her full attention.

"You remember Audrey?"

"Audrey. Audrey who?"

"Oh well you wouldn't know her surname but you remember the one I used to play cards with, the one with the dreary husband who always had grubby hands." Betty's excitement seemed to outweigh the statement.

For once the three of us were all in the same room. The gloriously spacious living room with its rich burnished tiles leading out onto the patio through open French windows. I had a pile of ironing to do and the light was best in here in the evenings. The sun streamed through the kitchen windows at the back of the house in the mornings and gradually worked its way round to the front late afternoon and early evening. The light reflected and bounced off the iron as I lifted it once more to iron perfect creases into Gerard's best white shirt.

Deirdre was sat in her favourite deep blue Ikea armchair angled in one of the open doorways so that the sun fell on the back of her neck. Betty had just flounced downstairs looking worryingly sprightly. Deirdre had noticed too. I tried to tip Betty the wink but she was too absorbed in her news.

"I think so mother. What about her?" Deirdre was looking puzzled.

I switched the iron off at the plug and muttered something about getting a drink.

"Does anyone else want one?" By this time I was stood in the kitchen doorway and managed to catch Betty's eye. I dropped my right shoulder. This, we had agreed, right at the beginning was going to be my warning signal if Betty was becoming too 'fit'. Normally Betty handled this very well with a gradual return to her weary state, but for some reason she ignored me. They both shook their heads at the drinks offer.

"Well she's just phoned me to say that she has left her dreary husband, bought herself a little flat in Guildford and has asked me to join her for Christmas." Betty took a breath.

Deirdre was rearranging herself in her chair uncrossing her long legs and folding her hands neatly on her lap. She always did this when she was about to launch into some convoluted explanation. All this of course gave Betty time to anticipate and deliver her decision.

"I told her, Audrey I said, these kids, sorry my family," Betty corrected herself as Deirdre shuddered." Have been wonderful to me, they've given me back my life. They deserve to have this Christmas to themselves. After all they've been together nearly five years and still no sign of grandchildren..." her voice faltered as she wondered if she'd hit the wrong note. I had retreated to the kitchen in fear of cracking up. I was sure those very same lines had been plucked from a Bette Davis movie that we watched last week.

The sound of Gerard's car crawling up the driveway provided a welcome diversion. We watched, all of us, mesmerised as he enacted his leaving- the - car ritual. He ejected the tape he was playing, after stopping it first. He placed it carefully back in its Perspex case and its rightful spot in the leather carrying case. The engine is still running, it needs to be, well at least the ignition still switched on so that he can close the windows. Deirdre allows herself a sly smile as we listen to Gerard turn off the engine. He wipes the arms of his glasses on a linen handkerchief which apparently he keeps for this sole purpose. I know because whenever I do the laundry his handkerchiefs are crumpled but never dirty! He places his glasses back into their brown Christian Dior case and into the breast pocket of his shirt. Unable to contain ourselves any longer, Betty, Deirdre and me burst out laughing. Fortunately Gerard is far enough away not to hear us. With one thump on the steering wheel, he has remembered. He switches on the ignition and closes the windows. We compose ourselves as he gets out of the car and retrieves his jacket from the hook behind him. His next car is going to have air conditioning, as soon as he can afford it. He does not believe in living beyond his means. Having the windows open with the traffic moving so slowly out of the city, just isn't enough anymore.

"Maman, you look well this evening," he says as he gives Deirdre her customary peck on the top of her head but looking at Betty.

"Yes she does doesn't she, better than she's looked in ages wouldn't you say Laura?"

Oh...Now I got it.

"Mother was just saying that an old friend in England has rung and invited her to go to over for Christmas." she said evenly, knowing full well what Gerard's reaction would be.

"Mais non Bettee...Christmas is for family, you know."

He sat down on the arm of his wife's chair, still holding his car keys in one hand and his jacket draped over the other. "Tell her Cheri."

This was going to be interesting.

"I'll just go upstairs for a while and let you talk." I offered. My room was directly above the living room.

To my surprise Betty said "No need, I want to ask you something as well." Curiouser and curiouser.

"What are you up to mother?"

This mother and daughter role reversal still amused us all so I played along.

"Yes Betty what's going on?" I asked pretending to be cross.

Gerard didn't get it. *Betty she is the movver and Deirdre is the daughter, non?* We had tried explaining. We weren't sure if it was a French thing or a man thing, in case it was the latter we gave up.

"Now you have to be honest with me okay?"

"Okay." I wasn't worried. I could tell by Betty's expression it was going to be something I liked.

She turned her attention to Deirdre. "You know how badly my legs swell, even after a short flight." We all nodded, "Well how about if I go back with Laura next week?" she paused and then produced her trump card, "Just think of the money it will save, you're already paying for the petrol and we can share a twin room en-route."

Although Gerard loved his mother in law deeply, he also loved the idea of there being some money left when she shed her mortal coil. Both Gerard and Deirdre feigned expressions of deep contemplation.

"Coffee anyone?" I had to say something; living in this Channel 4 soap opera was causing quiet, internal convulsions. They were not helped by Betty who was patiently waiting at the bottom of the stairs where she had stood all along holding onto the banister for support. She could be mistaken for someone who was at the vet's and was waiting to hear if her dog had to be put down.

"Yes please Laura." It was Gerard who broke the silence.

"I 'ave some work to do before we sleep."

His turn of phrase still made me smile. "Would you bring it up to my study please Laura."

It was a statement not a question. I had been tempted early on to remind him that I was not his secretary but then on contemplation I knew I had a 'good deal' with the Moulins and in any case if we were sharing a house you'd make coffee for each other, I reasoned...Still, there was something about the way he asked. Betty had noticed it straightaway.

"It's just his way. He's not comfortable with the situation. He's French. You're not family and you're not a work colleague. You're 'a friend' but also an employee. Give him time."

Betty gave me one of her smiles. The sort that over the coming months could have persuaded me to empty my Swiss bank account into her handbag...should I ever have one.

"Well I don't know Mother, you have put Laura in rather a spot." Deirdre tilted her head trying to read my body language from the kitchen.

"Honestly I don't mind but I have thought of one problem." I had to say it.

Betty glared at me. "Um, does anyone remember the state of my car when I arrived?"

For once Gerard was first to cotton on. "Ah. She is full!" he said wondering immediately if that was a good thing or a bad thing. In Gerard's mind everything had to be divided up, it couldn't just be. He did his Masters in Philosophy. He never stops analysing, Deirdre told me one day when I inquired if he was okay, after he had been staring at the largest cypress in the garden for about half an hour.

He was half way up the stairs and leaning over the banister holding his jacket at arm's length being careful not to crease it.

"Is there anything that could wait until the second week of January?" We all looked puzzled. He continued. "I 'ave the business meeting in London, I think it is..." he was searching through his Filofax "Yes, we 'ave the tenth of Janvier."

Of course he took no luggage except his suit bag...bingo! "Could a large suitcase full provide enough room for you and your luggage, Mother?" Inquired Deirdre waving her arms around apparently to indicate the overall size of a suitcase or her mother, I wasn't sure which.

"Remember I'm not taking the television back, it's on its last legs anyway. And that was on the passenger seat." I agreed.

Only Betty was silent as we found ways to evacuate her. Amazing considering 'her family' had been so against the whole idea a few moments ago.

ALL EXPENSES PAID

Monday 18th December

Back to reality via Folkestone.

"Yes, yes, we're driving off the cross channel ferry at four a.m. so that automatically makes us drug dealers."

"Now now madam, we're only trying to do our job!" Hands firmly on his hips, straight out of the 'How to intimidate people' handbook, the Customs guy leant into my open window, exuding 'don't hold the onions' breath. Yuk. I relented...a little. "I know, but I'm always getting stopped. I don't smoke and I hardly ever drink, why me?"

Up until that point I hadn't been tired and neither had Betty. A couple of night owls. Deirdre would be horrified. She's had two strokes you know. She needs her rest.

But now I was beginning to feel like I had indeed just driven six hundred and fifty miles. Perhaps we should have stayed somewhere after all, but we had agreed to save the money and find somewhere really nice back in England. "Well, I'm afraid you just happen to fit a suspect profile that we have. Sorry," he added.

The boring one was doing all the talking. The good looking one (I wondered if they did the good cop, bad cop routine) anyway, the good looking one would not make eye contact so I was getting bored as well as tired. Betty was feigning sleep; her theory being that we were less likely to be disturbed if they saw an elderly lady, snoozing. But even she had given up now.

"Look, are you going to search me or not?" Betty directed her ridiculously provocative request to the good looking one. She inclined her head, raising both eyebrows and licking her lips as she spoke.

"Just open the boot please madam."

It was less- than- handsome, onion breath who spoke.

Betty patted me on the back as I looked down to check my laces before hauling myself out of the car.

"See!" I volunteered. Onion breath motioned to his mate who came to stare in disbelief.

"Well?" I asked.

He slammed the boot shut and bade us on our way.

"Still want to drive?" I asked a nodding Betty.

"Hum, what dear?"

"Nothing, I was just saying we'll try Folkestone instead, it's not far."

Folkestone, five forty five a.m. A week before Christmas in an English seaside town or a blob on the landscape of the planet Desolation, you decide. Betty shifted in her seat and propped herself up against the headrest in our warm and dry car, as I pulled to a stop.

"Don't go away." I nudged her as I emerged from the car wrapping my old live-in-the-car , Highlander, mac around me. It was drizzling now, not real rain just enough to make you feel damp and uncomfortable, the sort of weather that makes you feel like screaming. If you're going to rain, get on with it. Instead I said. "Just seen a milk float, he should know if there is anywhere open. Won't be a minute."

I tried not to startle the milkman who was strangely whistling a Christmas carol, he sounded cheerful as if he was enjoying his job. I wasn't successful.

"Shite!" he hollered, steadying himself against a stack of crates. "You scared me 'alf to deaf." He clutched his chest, gathering up handfuls of regulation navy anorak. He wore a navy peak cap with white initials on the side. His name was either Donald & Gary or milkman's pay had increased considerably while I had been away.

"Sorry, but we've just arrived from France and really need somewhere to rest for a few hours. Do you know anywhere that might be open?" I gave him my best, forlorn smile, complete with Bambi eyes. He looked at me in much the same way as the Customs Officers had. "It's for me and my elderly Aunt" I added hopefully. This did the trick. Always have either a small child or elderly person at hand in times of need.

"You could try Miss Lawrence; she tends to get up pretty early. It's the Guest House at the end of that row of houses, over there." he said, pointing back the way we'd come. "Lovely view across the sea."

Oh sure, terrific, just like the South of France, how lucky can a girl get. Betty was sitting bolt upright by now and powdering her nose using her Elizabeth Arden compact. A powder compact, I'd had one in my early teens in a feeble bid to be grown up, but then those were the days when I had matching handbags and shoes and all the colours of the rainbow, not just black. I wondered how long it would take before the powder compact would disappear. Do the Spice Girls have them or will they go the way of other fashions and be relegated to the past waiting for their turn to come around again.

I parked the car at the side of the Guest House with the windscreen facing towards the garden, at the back. "Don't worry only three hours before the Post Office opens." Betty was trying to reassure me.

"Yes I know but by then I'll probably be fast asleep and I won't want to move."

Betty shrugged her shoulders in a way that had become part of daily life. I was missing it already. I had let my car tax run out before but not by three months. There had been a postal strike in France and EU, or not, you can't go into a French Post office and get car tax for an English registered car. There seemed to be a small golden glow coming from the back of the building, probably the kitchen.

"I'll go," says Betty springing from the car as if she had only just popped out to the local shops. "I'm less scary at this time of the morning."

I had told her about the milkman. She pulled her flowery silk scarf from around her neck and placed it lightly over her hair, very Royal Family. I climbed back into the car. I was at that, can't sleep, can't stay awake stage now, where every time you go to drop off, one of your legs jumps out in front of you. A sharp tap on the back of the car made me turn and knock my head on the window...Time to stop. It was Betty trying to open the boot.

****

Miss Lawrence eyed me suspiciously in the manner to which I was becoming accustomed.

"We can have a twin room for twenty five pound," pronounced Betty looking at me, willing me not to start bartering.

"That's the tariff for one night. There are no reductions."

Miss Lawrence folded her arms across the place where her chest would have been if she had had one. She looked as if she had never had a full English breakfast in her life. In fact I wasn't sure she had tried much of anything. She wore a calf length grey and pink spotted housecoat or was it an overall, it was hard to tell. Her long wispy grey hair was tied back into a bun secured with a tortoiseshell comb, which probably weighed almost as much as she did.

"Breakfast is between eight and nine in the breakfast room."

I had to blink to stay awake at this riveting news. She handed the key to Betty, indicating the stairs through an opaque glass door. "First floor, second door on the right."

The brown and cream carpet strip up the middle of the stairs was threadbare in places. We walked single file so as not to wake the other guests. Betty's heels on the wooden floor would have resounded around Folkestone. Room number seven and more of the same nineteen fifties' carpet.

"Hey this takes me back," said Betty fingering the pale lemon candlewick bedspread. "Oh dear," she added as several threads came away between her fingers. "Don't know that I fancy sleeping here."

"Hang on a minute, it might be okay underneath."

I volunteered, having a far better knowledge of cheap hotels than Betty did. "I usually get rid of the top cover straight away, it's so depressing, but there are usually clean sheets underneath." I rolled back the offending article "See, all freshly laundered. You just have to learn to ignore the grotty bits."

"Is this the kind of place you'd usually stay in?" Betty glanced at me. I swear for a moment that she looked at me as though I was a stranger. I went over and put my arms round her forcing her shoulders up into their usual shrug.

"Okay, point taken. What's the bathroom like? I always feel better after a shower."

I went in first, preparing an experienced Estate Agent patter in my head...traditional...original features...a certain charm...

"It's crap, Betty. Believe it or not I think a bath might be a better idea."

"Oh all right you run it and I'll get undressed."

I heard a heavy sigh as she plonked down on the bed.

The main overhead florescent tube cast an eerily even light around the room. The cracking vinyl on the floor, as multi coloured and patterned as the carpet offered up decades of dead human cells. Thank heavens for clean bath mats with a shiny backing so that you can skate around the floor without ever having to touch the hard, cold linoleum. The mirror above the basin was not kind; its silver backing was peeling off, leaving the onlooker with a sense of decrepitude. Perhaps this is how you look when you have leukaemia, my favoured disease of the week.

"What are you doing in there?" Betty's voice had taken on the tones of an old and irritated English woman. My god, is this what she was like before she went to France? She had told me something about her life before JL, as we called him between ourselves, but this reality was unnerving, I had to get her out of here as fast as possible.

"Ready Madam, your bathing chamber awaits."

I opened the door with a flourish. I stopped, I stared.

"Betty?" I asked "Blimey, you are a chameleon. You should have been a spy. "

I had never seen Betty look so drab. In fact I didn't know she was even capable of it. In all the six months that we spent together she had never looked her age; she did now.

"See why I had to get away? This was me five years ago." Betty tiptoed in her pink fluffy flat practical slippers and heavy cream dressing gown into the bathroom that I had prepared for her.

"I thought I could smell something." Betty glanced around the room. I'd switched off the main light leaving just a tiny glow over the mirror. Every flat surface I had covered with vanilla scented candles, Betty's favourite. The bath was full to the brim with bubbles catching the candle light, reflecting all the colours of the rainbow.

"Bless you Laura, what would I do without you?"

"Go on, get in and I'll bring you nice cup of tea." Betty looked suddenly frail. A word I had never associated with her before. I was tempted to offer my arm as she handed me her dressing gown but thought better of it. That would only serve to remind her of how she looked. I wanted the 'old' Betty back and fast.

"Have you checked to see if you have any messages?

"What dear?" Betty called through the bubbles.

"Messages, have you checked your phone since yesterday?"

"No I haven't. We've only been gone a day."

"Yes but I bet he's left you a message."

I stood holding the kettle in my right hand and firmly crossed my fingers on my left. If he hadn't called I had just made things worse.

"Go on then, you know how to work it better than I do." Betty lied, as I handed her a hospital green cup of tea courtesy of PG tips, and long life milk.

"Not a very good signal here, surprise, surprise." I scrolled through the messages or at least the numbers, I didn't want to read any messages that she'd saved, but there were no new ones. Damn.

"No new messages Betty but there was a missed call at eleven o clock last night."

"What's the number?" A glimmer of the old Betty came through the crack in the bathroom door.

"No number." I said and paused.

"Oh, okay. What are you doing? Are you going to have a dip after me?" Betty's tone was matter of fact.

"Yes I think I will. I'll get changed, go down for breakfast and then go to the Post Office, then have a couple of hour's kip. Are you going to have breakfast?"

"Might as well, seeing as we've got to pay for it."

Betty made it sound like the condemned man's last meal.

"Betty?" I asked popping my head around the bathroom door. "Do you know why there was no number registered with that missed call?"

She squinted at me, saying nothing.

"Well that always happens with International numbers."

I ducked just in time as the 'old' Betty returned and threw a sodden knot of pink flannel.

I turned round. "Landed on your bed Betty."

"Going to tell my daughter about you," exclaimed Betty, in a Minnie Mouse voice, for the zillionth time.

"And I might tell your daughter about you."

I stood in the doorway allowing my right shoulder to drop down.

****

"Do you have a copy of the Yellow Pages please?"

"Yes," came the reply. Miss Lawrence's eyes screwed up as she spoke. The excess powder gathered in lines on top of her cheeks. Her expression was full of suspicion. "What do you want it for?"

I wondered if my answer would either qualify or disqualify me from using it. Somehow I didn't think that a Tattoo Parlour would put me in the user's department.

"Just want to find a florist, Interflora, you know the kind of thing."

The expression softened, but the powder stayed in line. She pursed her lips as if blotting her lipstick for the umpteenth time.

"Just one moment," she said raising the forefinger on her right hand. One of those universal gestures I thought immediately reminded of Ed.

She walked back into her small dark office. It had a solid wooden door to the left and opaque sliding windows to the right. A notice, secured with curling sellotape read: Knock Loudly. BUT only in emergencies.' A blue - yellow light flickered beyond the frosted glass. I could hear a filing cabinet being unlocked, a drawer on its metal runners sliding out, and then clunking to a halt. What a performance. I began to wonder if it might be a first edition. There were two clicks as the cabinet was locked and the light deactivated.

Just as I suspected. Yellow Pages, pre-decimalisation. Oh well...

"Thanks." I said and started to walk towards the stairs.

"Oh, but you can't take it with you."

Obviously a particularly valuable edition.

"Um well I was only going to my room with it. I'll bring it straight back." I offered.

"Well, I'd rather you found the information you need and then I can put it straight back in the office. If you'd be so kind. Florists will be found towards the front."

I suddenly had a thought. "You're not related... I mean do you have a female relative living in Warwickshire?"

Naturally such as personal question was deemed unanswerable.

"Do you want this Yellow Pages or not? I do have other guests to attend to, you know."

"Yes I do. I won't be a minute." I turned my back and laid the truly yellowing pages on the hall table. Couldn't imagine there were many tattoo cum piercing places in Folkestone. Aah. Got it! I wrote down the address in the front of my diary.

I left Miss Lawrence bathing in the glow of my most grateful smile.

I walked up the middle of the stair carpet imagining the many weary travellers that had done the same, especially those poor deluded foreigners who had come in search of some Nirvana....Shouldn't the docks at Dover bear a sign...This country carries a Government Health Warning. Grey skies, grey landladies and brown Windsor soup. At least we knew what to expect but imagine some poor souls from Paris or Provence arriving here for their first taste of La vie Anglaise.

I pushed the door open gently. Betty had left it on the catch; it was less noisy that way. She was spark out on her bed still wrapped in her less than fluffy white towel. I didn't want to disturb her but knew she wouldn't like waking up lying on the dubious lemon woven blanket, so I took her burgundy wool dressing gown from the door and laid it across her and the bed, it was big enough. In fact it looked suspiciously like a man's, perhaps it was the one thing she had kept of her husband's. She had always described him as the slow homely type, not a bad person, just not right for her. I had never really found out what happened to him, although Deirdre certainly had different memories and instantly forbade her mother to talk about him whenever his name came up. You could almost see him encased in a swirl of pipe smoke as he eased himself into his matching Burgundy slippers.

It was as if Betty was living her life back to front. Perhaps that was what had drawn us together in the first place. Going against the grain, moving the goal posts. You can't do that at your age. We had both heard that one.

Grabbing my coat, I took the key and dropped the catch. I wasn't sure how long I would be. I knew the chances of Axel just happening to be this side of the channel were remote but I was already feeling the general malaise of winter, coupled with the fact that I had had more excitement in the last six months than I had in the last six years in England. Doom and gloom were the order of the day. At least the rain had stopped but the biting easterly wind had not dropped.

Monday 18th December.
Depressed already!

Just what had been in that sausage I wondered as it repeated on me again the moment I opened my mouth in the Post Office.

****

Not that I was in any position to complain. In France I had tried everything, because let's face it, they eat everything. If it stands still long enough for them to shoot it, then there has to be just the sauce recipe for it somewhere.

Betty had poked at her over cooked fried egg.

"Salmonella," I had reminded her.

"Don't think even Bubonic Plague would induce the French to over-cook anything," replied Betty.

We looked at each other and sighed.

"At least you're going back after Christmas." I prodded her shoulder with an egg free knife.

"Yes but what if Jean-Louis finds someone else while I'm away. A month is a long time for any man, but a Spaniard living in the South of France…"

Her voice trailed off, her eyes losing their sparkle as she stared into the middle distance, contemplating the worst.

****

An irritated cough from across the counter made me jump.

"You'll have to fill out one of these," said the friendly Post Office Counters Ltd lady.

"Can I have another please. Sorry."

I thought of explaining my dilemma...I've just driven from the South of France, so I'm tired... but would she care?

"I made a mistake...thank you."

My mouth forced a smile; my eyes were not so obliging.

I walked back to our hotel as fast as my legs would carry me. Drive up to the Post Office? No fear, I had got away with it this far I wasn't going to tempt fate by leaving my car in the main street of Folkestone. Walking back I marvelled at how much can change in a few hours.

"I don't think they actually imprison people for late car tax you know."

This had been Betty's advice at my paranoia.

"How would you know, you've lived in France long enough now, you've forgotten the whole way of life."

****

And to think we had been sitting at our favourite quayside bar in Martigues just forty eight hours earlier. The regulation BMWs, Porsche and Lotus accompanying the glistening yachts of varying sizes. The red ringed circle, the shoes with the line through them, strictly observed. I idly thought of buying one to send to Madam Sourpuss/ Belcher to display in her porch.

"Grand Marnier and chocolate sauce for me."

I had given up speaking French to Andre, he had spent so much time working in London he was hardly your typical French waiter.

"Same for me." Betty licked her lips.

"Crêpes, they're so simple to make, why don't we eat them in England, apart from Shrove Tuesday that is."

I was already in 'anti-all things English mode' and we hadn't even left yet. I folded yesterday's copy of the Mail over to read the weather forecast for the rest of the week. I wriggled my toes; free in their open toe shoes....back into boots for you in two days time.

****

I looked at Betty. She was 'off' somewhere too. I left her to her thoughts. Something beginning with JL no doubt. They had managed a quick farewell dinner last night. I dropped her off at the garage, something about JL's oily overalls, nothing surprised me anymore, while I went to the pictures. We'd tried to find a double feature or at least a film that Betty had seen before, but settled for the latest Hollywood comedy/romance so that a) I could explain it to Betty in two sentences and b) Deirdre wouldn't want to know about it anyway. I sometimes wondered if Betty and JL would ever tell Deirdre and Gerard or whether the subterfuge added too much excitement to the situation for them to ever change it. I was sad to be leaving. It had been one of the most educational times of my life, in every sense. But, as far as Deirdre was concerned I had performed my job and my contract was over. The last couple of weeks had been quite tense as a natural jealousy began to filter through each time Betty bemoaned my leaving.

"Really mother, don't be selfish. Laura has her own life to go back to in England."

ALL EXPENSES PAID

Thoughts of Julia and the expressions on her face when I told all that had happened. I could write a book, I told her one evening on the phone. You won't believe what Betty's been up to this week.

****

I managed to open the bedroom door without disturbing sleeping beauty. She had obviously woken at some stage because she was now snoring gently between the sheets. Her burgundy dressing gown was back hanging on the door. I noticed a glimmer of flickering green light from the window sill. Aah, she had been making a call on her favourite new toy, her English mobile phone. She had decided it was worth it, seeing as she was going to be staying at least a month.

Monday 18th December.

Meanwhile back at the 'Ritz' Folkestone.

God I was exhausted. I eased off my trainers, one foot with the other and sat down on my bed. I concertina-ed my jeans to my ankles and let them shuffle to the floor. Betty had thoughtfully turned down the corner of the top sheet, just as I had been doing for her over the last few months. It was a touching gesture. I felt tearful as well as tired. I was really going to miss my youthful companion. I will get into my pyjamas in a minute... I thought.

****

"So. Did you find Axel?"

Betty was already dressed in a conservative light grey tweed suit and lemon silk blouse. She leant over my bed as she spoke. A waft of L'air du Temps gently focused my senses.

"Sorry, what Betty?"

I rubbed my eyes before remembering I still had my make up on. Flakes of mascara peppered my cheeks.

"Axel, did you find him?" Betty gave me her benevolent look.

"Oh, oh crikey I forgot to look. I was so tired and so relieved to get my car sorted I forgot."

"Ah, well, another time maybe..."

"Have you been up long?"

"No, just decided I couldn't relax properly here. I've had four hours sleep; that will do me for now."

"Okay I'll just get dressed and we can be on our way."

"I'll drive. Okay?" Betty straightened up a she spoke, looking every bit in control of the situation.

"Said you could." She certainly looked better than I felt . "What time is it anyway?"

"1.30. Shall we get out of here and grab some lunch somewhere?"

"Good idea Betty, me old mate."

I pulled on my old jeans, now well and truly crumpled. I felt really shabby next to Betty.

****

"I sometimes wonder who looks after whom?" exclaimed Betty, tapping the windscreen of my trusty old Renault 5. Out of habit she was about to get into the passenger seat when she said, "Laura?"

"Yes Betty?"

"Just what have you been stressing about for the last few days?"

"Oh, my God, wouldn't that have been so ironic, after all my efforts!"

"Here, give it to me, I'll put it in its little pouch." Betty placed the tax disc in its plastic holder.

"Just as well you're going to drive." I sighed.

We swapped sides and checked the clock in the car. "One forty five. We can't go far if we want some lunch," I muttered miserably remembering the two-o-clock curfew on food.

"Ah, but maybe I know somewhere that serves lunch until three –o- clock!" Betty preened, lifting her chin as if pointing the way. Betty was obviously so happy behind the wheel that for the first time in twenty four hours I sat back and relaxed.

"Here we are, Rutherfield. Think you'll like this place." Betty turned off the ignition and tapped my hands resting on my lap. "Wakey, wakey..."

"Oh Betty, this looks nice, have you been here before did you say?"

"Many times, but mainly during the summer. C'mon, shake a leg. I'm starving."

For one moment I remembered what I liked about England, village pubs and this one was picture postcard perfect. Set on the edge of a thriving small village, it was complete with a thatched roof and leaded light windows. The car park was almost full, Volvo's. Saab's and Mercedes...Aah...Sussex. I adjusted my jeans and zipped up my fleece jacket.

"Sorry Betty, I look a right scruff, next to you."

"I forgive you." Betty had a mysterious smile about her, the sort usually reserved for naughty school boys. It was all part of her charm, just when you thought you knew what she was going to do she'd surprise you with something completely different. I could see why Jean -Louis was taken with her. I hoped he would phone soon. Or maybe he had. Maybe that's what she was smiling about. All the right sounds and smells were coming from inside. I pushed open the heavy oak door and let Betty walk in ahead of me. The usual miniscule hallway provided Ladies to the left Gents to the right. A sepia photo of the pub circa 1878 hung proudly over the entrance to the lounge. A cacophony of clinking glasses, polite laughter and clunking billiard balls greeted our entrance. A real log fire in the corner provided one the most welcome sights so far. A middle aged (older than me) couple were getting up to leave. The fire looked inviting.

"Betty, do you want to grab those seats and I'll get the food."

I was worried about the time, it was ten to three.

I leant on the bar, the stools in these places are always a bit of a nightmare for me, even when I can get on successfully I nearly always have trouble with my dismount.

"Um, excuse me, are you still serving food?"

Funny how you can suddenly become absolutely ravenous the moment the chance of food is taken away. The girl (younger than me) behind the bar although stood directly in front of me, seemed to visiting some distant planet. I could see our precious minutes passing away. I glanced back at Betty who was 'playing' with her mobile phone. I tried again. "Excuse me! Please say you're still doing food. I'm with my elderly Aunt and we've just driven from Folkestone and we're, well, starving…"

With a sudden shake of her long wavy brown hair, she spoke. "Oh, goodness, I'm soo…sorry. Food yes, of course, the menu!" She said with a flourish, brandishing two, very thick brown leather bound copies, embossed with gold lettering.

"Um. I don't think we'll have time to read all this, what do you recommend?"

"Steak and Ale pie, best thing they do," she added in such a way that I wasn't sure whether this meant the rest was rubbish or…oh good grief, I was turning into Gerard! ...analysing everything...perhaps it was just as well I had left when I did. Betty had put away her new toy and was looking around the room appreciatively. I was loath to interrupt whatever memories were being relived, so I just mouthed to her...Steak and Ale pie? She nodded contentedly. And a bottle of red? She mouthed back. I tutted silently and shook my head. I raised my arms to mimick her driving. She pursed her lips into that little girl pout that I had seen work so often with JL...she mimed back...just a small one...her thumb and forefinger poised in mid air.

"Do you do wine by the glass?" I asked the extremely patient barmaid. She nodded, holding up first one then two fingers. I nodded and held up two fingers.

"Two Steak and Ale pies and two glasses of house red."

"Thank you dear, very much." Betty smiled radiantly at the girl, who jumped as if woken from a dream.

"Ooh, I thought you didn't...couldn't...erm speak..."

Betty and I turned, puzzled, to look at each other and all three of us saw the funny side at the same time. Up until that moment, the place could have been described as, calm, genteel, relaxing. All of us bursting out laughing however soon changed all that.

"If you don't mind me asking, where were you earlier, you seemed miles away."

The long brown wavy hair, now that it had appeared from behind the bar was almost down to her waist. She wore a long black skirt, short white lace edged apron and leather ankle boots identical to some I had worn last winter. The white t shirt showed evidence of a recent tan. "Mauritius, just got back yesterday..." her voice drifted off, due south. Betty and I nodded, understanding, in unison.

"Enjoy your meal both of you."

"Holiday or work do you reckon?" Betty turned to me. We were soon back into playing our favourite game. Guess the job /age/straight/gay/class/married/sinlge? So I asked her.

"Working in a hotel. It's a beautiful place. Ever been?" Sasha (we'd heard the barman call her) had come to clear away the plates and Betty using her perfectly good voice had asked the question. We both shook our heads. "Back here for Christmas?" I asked

"Yes, see my family, you know the sort of thing."

Sasha gave us both a quick glance, wondering if we were related.

Betty roared with laughter. "I'm here to get away from mine!"

I pretended to look hurt. Poor Sasha looked puzzled.

"It's okay, we're not related." I had to put her straight.

"Pudding?" Sasha offered.

"Not for me, just coffee please." I was feeling tired, bloated and generally knackered. As tempting as it was, spotted dick would have to wait for another day.

"Apple pie and custard please Sasha." Betty grinned.

"That's two lots of pastry Betty."

Betty stuck out her tongue.

"Are you sure you two are not related?" Sahsa tucked her pencil behind her ear as she walked back to the bar.

"You're not a brickie." We heard the barman say as he removed the offending article and placed it in Sasha's apron pocket.

The apple pie looked delicious but I knew it would just send me off to sleep and we still had the rest of our journey to do.

"That's a point. Betty, your friend's not expecting us until tomorrow. Where are we going to stay tonight?" Betty for once looked genuinely guilty. I had become an expert over the last six months. "Ah yes, good point." Betty stroked her chin in her usual nervous way, when she was trying to come up with a good answer.

"Betty, is there something you want to tell me?"

Betty put an overfull spoon to her mouth. Custard dripped back into the dish.

"B e t t y..?"

She avoided my gaze and motioned to Sasha to come over.

"Is the pie okay?" she looked concerned.

"What? Oh yes fine dear, but I was just wondering would you mind just standing there for a moment while I explain something to Laura, I think she might hit me..."

Sasha looked at me and shook her head. I shrugged. We both looked at Betty.

"Well, you know my friend who invited me over for Christmas?"

"The one in Guildford," I added, for Sasha's benefit.

"Yes, well, I've been trying to call her for the last few days and there's been no answer."

ALL EXPENSES PAID

"Well, maybe as she's not expecting you until tomorrow..." I stopped in my tracks as I saw Betty crossing her fingers. "Betty. Out with it."

Sasha glanced back at the barman as if assistance may be required at any moment.

"Well, you know Jean-Louis is going to Spain for Christmas and I couldn't really go with him and I just didn't fancy another traditional Franglais extravaganza..." Betty's voice had gradually gone up and up, finishing in a mouse- like squeak.

"Your English friend never did phone did she?" I didn't know whether to laugh or cry. Sasha was called back to the bar. We both agreed it was safe for her to retreat. Betty was shaking her head. "I thought she's bound to be there, she never goes away at this time of year. She wouldn't have minded..."

Minded?" I asked. "Yes; us just turning up like this..."

Monday 18th December

Room at the Inn

The three remaining customers were all sat on stools up at the bar; they all jumped as Betty's mobile rang to the tune of Jingle Bells.

"I thought you didn't know how to change the ring tone?" I looked at Betty suspiciously.

"I didn't do it; it was JL's idea of a joke. He said at least I'd remember him every time my phone rang."

Betty held the phone at arm's length, trying to read who was calling her, maybe it was her friend, she thought. "Hello?" Betty said ponderously, she was still amazed by her new gadget.

"Dahling." Panic opened her eyes wide, even more panic made her say, "What dahling, it's a terrible line, I mean signal, can't hear you very well. Can you call me in about fifteen minutes, I'm sure that will be better. Byee..."

Betty snapped the phone shut, put in down on the small round oak table and turned to me, all in one movement. "Heavens Laura, where are we supposed to be?" Betty was pointing at my coffee as she spoke. Sasha, who had been polishing glasses, one by one as they emerged from the dishwasher had also had one eye on us. She held up two fingers, we both nodded. I was beginning to think I would need more than strong coffee.

"Let's think, it's mid afternoon, well an hour later, say four thirty and we're still in France heading for the overnight ferry from Le Harve. We'll say we've just stopped on the motorway, we needn't be too specific. The small case of modern technology shook on the table as it rang. I answered it. I hate Jingle Bells.

"Deirdre. Yes we're both fine. Yes Betty's just gone to powder her nose."

I knew I was tempting fate when I used one of Betty's favourite expressions. I put my hand over Betty's mouth to stop her usual retort of, 'some people have noses in the funniest places…'

"Yes we found a very good chambre d'hotes, yes very reasonable. Betty by now was grimacing as if she just swallowed something very unpleasant. Sasha placed two coffees on the table. I nodded our appreciation. Turning away slightly she ripped off the top sheet of her order pad and placed it strategically between the two of us.

Betty smiled at the modern diplomacy.

"Do you want to talk to your mother?"

Betty was performing semaphore that would have made any girl guide proud." She should be back at any moment." I teased. "Oh okay, yes that's true, peak time. I will. I'm sure she'll phone you from her friend's sometime tomorrow. Yes I will, don't worry. Bye Deirdre."

Betty had sat back in the comfortable velvet banquette and was sipping her coffee.

"Very good," she said, patting me on the back.

"So what do we do now?" Betty beamed at the last customers to leave. She liked to 'connect' with everyone. She had read about it in one of her latest books, more friends, less enemies, she pronounced simply. Her part in world peace.

"You tell me, you're the one with nowhere to go."

Sasha was picking up the white and red rimmed saucer with Betty's credit card on it.

"I hope you won't mind me saying this, but did you say you need somewhere to stay for the night?"

Not quite four-o-clock but it was getting dark, I really didn't feel like driving and I was sure I shouldn't let Betty.

"Do you know of somewhere nearby?"

Betty nodded as I looked to her for confirmation.

"My parents, they run the B and B, only they call it a Guest House and they were saying this morning that no-one was arriving until tomorrow. Hang on let me just give them a quick call. Um...two singles?" She hesitated as she tried to remember just how many rooms they had. They'd taken on the place just as she had left for Mauritius.

"Anything. twin, double, whatever you have. That would be wonderful." Betty was waving her arms around again. I wondered why she never seemed to get tired.

ALL EXPENSES PAID

Monday 18th December

The milky bars are on me!

"Julia? Yes it's me. We're in a little village not far from Tunbridge Wells... No we won't get to Guildford until tomorrow. Are you? Really? Excellent, well why don't you come and join us?"

I put my hand over the phone and turned to Betty who was admiring the rose patterned quilt cover on her bed.

"This is more like it," she mused.

"Betty do you mind if Julia joins us in the pub tonight for a drink, only she's not far away and I'd love her to meet you."

"Of course. Why not?" Betty was hanging her burgundy dressing gown on the back of the bathroom door.

There was a tap on the door, Betty went to open it.

"Everything okay? I'm just off to get some sleep, jet lag, you know how it is. Do you think you'll be over to the pub later or mum wondered if you'd like some sandwiches in your room, we don't normally, but if you'd..."

Before Sasha could finish Betty had jumped in, hopping from foot to foot.

"No need. One of Laura's friends is coming along tonight, so we'll all be there."

Sasha shook her head, as she closed the door, the way I had done, repeatedly, when I first met Betty.

"See you later," I called out. It was coming up to five o clock and Betty was lifting her portable radio out of her suitcase.

"It's funny isn't it, the things you miss?" Betty placed the miniature silver Sony radio on the window sill, and extended the aerial.

"Sorry Betty, what were you saying?"

"Oh, just the Radio 4 news, one of the few things that I miss."

She reached up to fondle the saint Christopher on a chain that JL had given her the day before she left.

"I'm going to have forty winks Betty, how about you?"

"Probably," she said poking the ear piece into her left ear. The lead didn't reach from the window sill so she moved the radio to her bedside table.

Yes; this was definitely, more like it, I thought as I looked round the twin bedded room. Freshly decorated in a pastel shade of lemon, not unlike my room...oh dear...my room, the one I had lived in for the last few months, the one that I would probably never see again. A tear slipped down my cheek as I rolled over quietly to look at Betty, who was silently nodding to whatever piece of news she had just heard. What an adventure it had all been. I set the alarm for seven thirty, give us time to freshen up before going over to the pub and meeting Julia. I had given her the address of where we staying just in case we both became comatose and didn't show up.

A loud bang from downstairs interrupted my vivid dream, one I will be going back to later with a bit of luck. I decided it was the front door closing. The wind had got up while we were asleep and the house was beginning to sound its age. Still there were no creaks or groans from Betty, she was in the bathroom humming White Christmas.

Even I was getting into the Christmas spirit now.

"Betty, have you tried ringing your friend again yet?"

"Sorry what? Can't hear you, I'm just going into a tunnel..."

"Ha, ha, very funny."

"Still no answer. But we could just drive up there tomorrow. I know where she always leaves a key." Betty poked her head round the bathroom door as she spoke.

"Don't tell me; underneath the pot of geraniums to the left of the front door." I laughed.

"In December Laura? We'll never make a gardener out of you, will we? No. At her neighbour two doors down, who I happen to know quite well."

She had that smile again. I accepted that she had lived twice as long as me but she seemed to have three times as many memories.

"Well okay, if you're sure."

****

Sasha was already behind the bar when we walked in. She saw us and indicated the reserved sign on the table we had vacated only a few hours earlier. She had her hair tied up and secured with three combs, a couple of lose tendrils falling either side framing her face. I thought of the future impossibility of her becoming the landlady in Folkestone.

"Penny for them?" Betty nudged me back into the smoky warmth of The Jug and Hare.

"Oh just daydreaming, nothing really, I..."

"Laura!" Julia's voice ricocheted round the room and everyone turned to look.

"Julia my old mate!"

Betty stood aside to allow the two of us to fling ourselves across the gap between the bar and the door. "And this of course is Betty." Julia shot her hand forwards and grabbed her by the right hand. I had forgotten just how forceful she was. Must be all those dealings with horses; have to show them who is boss. She did a quick appraisal of Betty, head to toe.

"You weren't kidding were you Laura?"

Betty wasn't sure what to make of Julia, so I stepped in.

"Looks fabulous doesn't she?"

"If either of you says, for my age, I'm going to scream." Betty eyed us both hesitantly. It was the first time she had met any of my friends I realised. In all the time I had known her she had always called the shots, and now suddenly she seemed unsure of herself.

"Never," I said moving to her side and giving her a hug. "Julia my old best friend, meet Betty, my new best friend."

Betty was beginning to look tired and for a moment I felt irresponsible. It was so easy to forget Betty's age and the fact that she had had one stroke, albeit a minor one, eighteen months ago.

"C'mon, let's all sit down, over by the fire." I led the way.

Sasha was right behind. "What will it be ladies?"

"G and T for me please." Betty was always first to reply, in any bar.

"Julia, are you driving tonight?"

Betty threw her head back and screamed with laughter.

"Oh my god, she does it to you as well. Does she 'mother' all her friends?"

The pact was formed. Julia and Betty were immediate allies. "Well, she tries..."

"Oi! I'm only concerned and being practical." I defended myself.

As usual Sasha was the model of patience.

"Wondered if we could share a bottle of wine, that's all." I suggested.

"Let me see now, where is it I'm staying tonight, what was the name again?" Julia gave Sasha a sideways smile.

Sasha nodded. "Mum and Dad are thrilled with me, three paying guests. I'm going to ask for commission."

"Sash." It was the barman. Whilst we had been talking, a group of evening trippers had piled through the door behind us and were waiting anxiously at the bar.

"Oops, bottle of red please Sasha." I said.

****

It had been a lovely evening. I just had the Dover sole and salad followed by coffee, which was okay but not a patch on Andre's special blend, but it would do. On the one hand it seemed strange for the bar to be closing at eleven o clock but it was probably just as well as we both needed a proper night's sleep. The heavy hum of chatter had died down to a gentle pocket of sound over by the bar. Outside a car drove past, there was something different about it...somehow. A quick blast of Jingle Bells, blaring out of an over ambitious audio system, made Betty reach for her bag. We smiled. Julia hadn't noticed. Betty rested her hands back on the table.

"Mummy says, time for bed." I laid a hand on Betty's right shoulder. Her head jerked forward with fatigue. "Quick Julia, before we have to carry her." I added.

"Cheeky monkeys..."

But Betty really was looking whacked. She would have a lie in and breakfast in bed in the morning even if I had to cook it myself, I decided.

Another car whooshed past outside.

Julia caught my eye. "Are you thinking what I'm thinking?"

We got up together, forgetting Betty for a moment. Julia dashed towards the door ahead of me and flung it open. Sasha, behind the bar, looked up in surprise. Julia came back in before I had chance to see for myself, arms spread wide she bellowed "I'm dreaming of a white Christmas..."

"Really?" Sasha dumped her tea towel on the bar and ran to the window next to where we were sitting. Pulling the heavy green velvet curtain back revealed small arcs of white forming in the bottom left hand corners of the leaded light panes.

'Jingle Bells...jingle bells...' There it was again. Only this time it wasn't a passing car.

"Betty. Your phone." I shrieked.

"Oh, oh...gosh...yes...um...hello?"

Julia and I watched as Betty's face lost every trace of tiredness. Colour that had drained from her cheeks during the day miraculously re-appeared. Her shoulders went back as her head bent forward and to one side. The...hmmm's...were punctuated with...Oui....Oui...and Je sais.

Even Sasha had noticed the change and raised her eyebrows questioningly at me. I went over to the bar. Julia followed.

"Her Spanish lover...calling from France." I tried to sound nonchalant.

"Blimey!" Julia and Sasha said almost in unison.

Betty looked up "Jean-Louis says hi. He wanted to speak to you but I won't let him."

I sat down again, we could be a while. Even at home, well in France, he could be on for twenty minutes and that was when they were going to meet each other later. Try finding an Englishman who can talk for that long, with or without a phone. Sasha had finished behind the bar and was waiting to lock up, but patient as ever she sat down with me and Julia while Betty cooed into her tiny mobile phone.

"What!" she suddenly said, making us all jump. "Sorry" she looked at us, putting her hand over the phone. "It's JL, having a little joke..."

Turning away from us again she spoke into the phone with her hand round it like a school girl with a secret formula.

"Well okay, just a minute, here you are." Betty passed the phone to me "He wants to speak to you."

I leaned over to take the phone from her searching her eyes for some clue as to what was going on.

Sasha asked "Betty, are you feeling okay?" Betty nodded and just pointed towards me. I put the phone to my ear.

"What?" I echoed Betty a few seconds earlier. I stared at Betty with a mixture of disbelief and excitement. Sasha and Julia were almost on top of me trying to hear what on earth Jean-Louis was saying.

"And what did she say?" I asked Jean-Louis. "She did?" I screamed with laughter. "Okay, yes, here you are."

I handed the phone back to Betty.

"Well?" Julia had stood up and had her arms folded in front of her. "What's going on?"

"Ssh, hang on let Betty tell you."

I was grinning so much it hurt.

"And have you ever seen snow?" Betty was asking Jean-Louis as if the rest of the conversation had not taken place. "Well I don't see why, they weren't at the first one." Betty roared at her own joke. She reached into her handbag to retrieve a tiny triangular lace handkerchief. She dabbed her eyes. They were tears of laughter. The barman turned off the lights over the snooker table and draped tea cloths over the pumps.

"First time we've had an eighty year old at a lock-in." He snickered as he let himself out of the back door. "Night Sash."

"Night Ben. I'll lock up."

"Okay my little...erm...they're all listening, cheeky girls...bisou dahling...I will. Ciao..."

Betty flipped the phone and placed it back in her handbag, clunking it shut before she spoke.

"Are we really having a lock-in?" she directed her question to Sasha.

"Aren't you exhausted?" she asked.

"Not now I'm not." Betty glanced at me.

I glanced at her.

"I'm getting married. Jean-Louis has asked me to marry him!"

"Wow." Was all Sasha could manage.

"Gosh." Julia volunteered.

"The milky bars are on me." Betty leaped out of her seat and over to the bar, "I've always wanted to say that." she said in mock seriousness. Grabbing the nearest tea cloth she flung it over her head and started to sing... "I'm getting married in the morning..." punctuated by "I'm dreaming of a White Christmas...." at which point Betty pointed to me. I joined in. Julia and Sasha accompanied us with Jingle Bells.

"Champagne!" cried Sasha, lifting the phone off its hook.

"Mum, get Dad, come over to the pub, back door, we're having a little celebration...what?...Oh just come...tell you when you get here."

She hung up and went to unlock the door as she assembled six glasses and put them on a tray.

"Only the finest; whatever you've got." Betty said in answer to Sasha's question.

George and Hester appeared, somewhat bewildered, in the kitchen doorway. Sasha shooed them round the bar and handed them each a glass of Bollinger.

"Mum, Dad, this is Betty and she has just been proposed to." Sasha raised her glass towards Betty. Hester looked around the room, obviously expecting the groom.

"On the phone." I added seeing their confusion.

"To Betty and Jean-Louis." I cheered .

"To Betty and Jean-Louis." The chorus rang out. We all turned as a tiny ember in the fading log fire suddenly burst into full flame reflecting in the already empty champagne bottle on the silver tray.

Monday 18th December.

Endings and beginnings.

"But what about Deirdre and Gerard, won't they be gutted. I mean they don't even know he exists."

We were back in our room. Betty was cleansing her face in the bathroom; I was sat at the dressing table mirror. We both threw tissues into the bin.

Betty stopped and said. "Laura you know how old fashioned they can be. I just want everything to be simple, perfect and spontaneous. It's what keeps me young," she added winking at herself in the mirror.

She pinched the skin underneath her chin and waited for it to spring back...She sighed.

"We have to grab happiness when we can, you know that."

"I know, I know, but I still think your daughter will be hurt knowing that I'm here and she's not."

I was torn between what I thought was the right thing and what I *felt* was the right thing...oh hell...it's that Gerard again...and how come? I hardly ever spoke to him, or maybe I had always been like it and only now saw my own reflection.

"Ah, well, I've already thought of that. There will be two lots of photographs. Some with Laura and some without." Betty preened as she massaged throat cream into her neck with deft upward movements.

"My god, you worked that out already?" I was amazed.

"I might not be so quick on my feet but the mind you know..." Betty glided from the bathroom to her bed and sat down on the end, turning to face my back. I looked at her through the mirror.

"It's simple. Jean-Louis is flying over tomorrow, first flight he can get and then we'll be married the day after."

"But this close to Christmas, where will you find anywhere?" I was all for spontaneity but this seemed pretty impossible, even with Betty's determination.

"Ah well, you remember the neighbour, two doors down from my friend's?"

"I do...oops, sorry that's your line..."

"Yes dear, highly amusing. Well he just happens to owe me a favour and luckily he is a vicar and he will be around."

"So, good grief, what are you going to wear. Can I give you away?" I laughed as I fingered the collar of my towelling dressing gown as if it were a gentleman's jacket.

"We'll go shopping tomorrow and Jean-Louis suggested that you be best man but no speeches, thank you."

Jingle bells......jingle bells. "Hello?" said Betty fishing the phone out of her bag. "No, that's fine, no, not yet. Tired yes, we are...... very." Betty shook her head as I mouthed JL at her. Audrey, she mouthed back at me.

"Ooh..." I said, climbing in between perfectly new, white Egyptian cotton sheets.

Bliss. I could sleep for a week, if I wasn't so excited.

ALL EXPENSES PAID

"Are you sure, really Audrey? That would be wonderful...No he doesn't know yet. I'll phone him first thing in the morning. You know how he always goes to bed early in the winter...Oh I know and I want to hear to all about you ...you didn't move...no didn't think you would...There is just one other thing...yes I know we can talk tomorrow but I am going to be rather busy."

I had started to doze so I felt for the bedside lamp and pressed the switch. I vaguely heard Betty trying very hard to suppress her girlish giggles as she dived under the sheets to tell Audrey her news.

Tuesday 19th December

Meet the vicar.

As a special concession Hester agreed we could have breakfast in bed. It arrived at eight thirty, as requested, complete with a handmade 'congratulations' card on Betty's tray. George laid my tray on the dressing table, as I was still only capable of opening one eye, let alone sit up.

"Thank you George, you're very kind. Thank Hester too."

He nodded to us both and backed out of the room. I felt like royalty. Betty handed me a glass of fresh orange juice off my tray. "Ta." I said gratefully propping myself up on one elbow.

"I presume you have a plan, my dear Watson?" I blinked, trying to shake off the feeling of sleep that seemed to be dragging my eyelids down.

"Bien sur, my young friend. It goes like this."

Jingle bells...jingle bells."Guess who?" asked Betty, looking at me before answering the phone.

I was out of bed now and capable of walking to the dressing table to eat my breakfast...just...but still too sleepy to engage in conversation.

"Dunno Betty, who?"

Probably the Archbishop of Canterbury. Heard Betty's news and would love 'to do' their wedding. No problem.

Betty chuckled as she answered her phone. " It certainly is...ooh ...Audrey told you...wait till I get hold of her...you will?...you're a dahling...No, she doesn't know yet...of course I'm going to tell them...don't start...What? Okay. See you at ten. Then I have to go shopping for a dress, byee."

Betty flipped her phone shut in her usual manner.

"You're going to unhinge that phone before it's much older." I said through a mouthful of toast.

"That," said Betty "was Deirdre's father!"

"Blimey, don't tell me he's coming to the wedding."

I choked as a larger than usual piece of toast went down. I grabbed at my coffee and took a gulp.

"Oh he'll be there." Betty smirked. "In fact..." *Jingle bells...*

"Hello dahling... yes of course I guessed it was you...mother's intuition...how are you...and Gerard...and the weather...oh you've heard..?"

I looked up but I couldn't see the expression on Betty's face.

"Betty!" I hissed....quietly.

"Yes, quite a covering this morning."

She turned and pointed at me, shaking her head from side to side. "Lovely dahling...yes , back in time for a white Christmas...Laura's headed off already...Yes...I know, I shall miss her too...yes she went early this morning in case the snow gets any worse..."

I sat at the dressing table shaking my head and pointing at the end of my nose, extending my index finger, impersonating Pinocchio.

Betty waved at me, dismissively, laughing.

****

"I'll drive, I know the way. Okay?" Betty held out her left hand for the keys. It wasn't really a question. There was no stopping her now.

"Can we get there by ten o clock?" I wondered, checking my watch.

"That's why I want to drive, there are a few short cuts that I learnt, to avoid the hold ups, especially around Gatwick."

"Isn't petrol expensive here?" Betty was leaning out of the window as I shook the last drops into the tank. "That enough?" she said squinting at the gauge. She had taken off her glasses the minute we pulled into the service station. *I don't mind wearing them when I'm driving, but I might see someone I know once I'm stationary.*

How will you know? I rejoined.

Vanity; I called it. Pride in one's appearance, Betty said.

I took the twenty pound note she was waving and headed for the cash till. I hesitated by the magazines and walked on. Was I cured? Could I redeem my subscription to magazines-aholic.

I felt Betty's eyes searching me out as I reappeared through the automatic door.

****

"Ever wondered if you had a previous life as a rally driver or has JL been teaching you a few tricks?" I held onto my seat as Betty took the next corner mainly on two wheels. Perhaps she was related to Zigo! Ever since seeing *Six Degrees of Separation*, I had been intrigued by the idea that we were all really connected in some way.

I tried to concentrate on the tree lined lanes, stripped of their summer foliage covered with a scattering of white frost. We turned onto the A25 and into a tailback of traffic.

"Almost there." Betty smiled as she dropped the car into neutral. I couldn't complain. It was a bad habit we shared.

"Have you ever driven Jean-Louis's car?" I asked as the cars in front slowly began to move. She found first gear as she answered. "Oh yes; lots of times."

Oh well, one more thing to know about Betty. For a moment I felt sad. How will Deirdre feel when she finds out that her mother has been leading a double life...How will she react...How would she feel about me meeting her father..? I had imagined what he might be like, but it was going to be strange to finally put a face to my thoughts.

I grabbed the dashboard as we swerved sharply to the left.

"Ooh, sorry. The hedge is a lot higher than the last time I was here. I almost missed it."

Betty turned off the ignition as we glided to a halt in the gravel driveway.

"The Rectory?" I looked at Betty "But it's ten fifteen. I thought we were going straight to..."

"Angel!" boomed a voice from the right of the car.

"I'm not dead yet, Bernard." Betty quickly removed her glasses.

"I can see that. You look wonderful." Bernard had lifted the handle on the driver's door and was extending his arm.

"And you must be Laura." Bernard nodded to me as I emerged from the passenger seat.

"Come in, come in. Coffee's ready. Proper coffee, don't worry. I sent Cecil out the moment I knew you were back." he said with pride.

Deirdre's Father.

Tuesday 19th December.

"You had red hair," I exclaimed, picking up a photo of Betty which took pride of place on the grand piano. "Sorry...erm...hope you don't mind?"

I bit my lip as I looked from one to the other.

"Bit younger then."

Betty smiled at Bernard as she took the heavy silver frame from me.

Cecil appeared with a tray of coffee. I automatically held out my arms to take the tray. "Ooh, a kindred spirit," said Cecil. "No need, but thank you," he added with a flourish.

"Betty darling, how are you?" Cecil greeted Betty with a peck on each cheek.

"Go on, you tell her."

Bernard was looking at Betty who was watching Cecil poor coffee into tiny dark green, gold rimmed cups. "The poor girl must be wondering what the hell is going on."

"Language Bernie." Cecil mocked as he ran his finger around an imaginary 'dog collar.'

It was true but I was partly mesmerised by the opulent surroundings. A Georgian exterior in the heart of the stockbroker belt and an Art Deco interior. I immediately wondered if Gerard had been here, he'd love it. And that had to be Lalique on the fireplace.

"So. Yes. Just what is going on?"

I brought my gaze back to rest on Betty. Bernard indicated the two opposing white sofas. The four of us sat down. I was terrified of spilling my coffee, so left it on the table in front of me, at least until after whatever they had to tell me.

"Well? A girl can die of suspense you know," I demanded.

"I think that's cats." Cecil offered solemnly.

"That's curiosity," yelled Bernard. "Sorry," he placed his cup back in its saucer with a clang as he spoke.

I made a small growling sound, which Marge Simpson would have been proud of.

Jingle bells....jingle bells.

"I don't believe it!"

I looked at the men's bemused faces as Betty reached into her bag.

"Oui Cheri...Of course...What time?...Perfect...Ah yes, good point, I expect so. Can I call you right back?...Bisou...That was Jean-Louis." declared Betty.

"Really?" said Bernard. "You do surprise us."

I snatched Betty's phone out of her grasp. "Tell me what's going on or Jingle Bells here gets it."

I gently played with the flap.

"Okay, okay. She's been like this the whole six months. Bossy,bossy,bossy."

Betty grinned, batting her eyelashes.

"You said..." Bernard glanced at me sympathetically. He was almost as I had imagined. A clerical version of Father Christmas. A head of pure white hair and an immaculate bristly moustache. At a little over six foot and doe like brown eyes. Dark brown corduroy trousers and cream cashmere polo neck jumper.

I could see Deirdre straight away.

"Let me introduce Deirdre's father and his companion Cecil. Bernard is Rector in this parish and will marry me and JL as soon as he can get here. You owe me one don't you dear....?"

"I do. And a promise is a promise."

Bernard stopped as he realised the faux pas he had just made.

"Or not," added Cecil with an air of exasperated surprise. The three of them burst out laughing.

"What now?" I asked getting irritated at being left out.

"Sorry Laura, but you see there was one promise I didn't keep. The one to marry Deirdre's mother. I mean, me and her, not to someone else, I wasn't a priest then."

"Thank goodness you plan your sermons better than this," said Cecil, as he handed me my coffee. "Drink up, it will get cold. Basically Laura, old Bernard here wasn't exactly a saint in those days. He loved Betty. Who wouldn't?"

Betty smiled in acknowledgement. "But he had to choose between her and the church."

"Oh I see." My hand shook as I put my cup back on the large oval glass coffee table.

"Sorry Laura, but I do have to phone JL back before he gets his flight. Bernard, how would you feel about the groom staying here tonight, if he can get the six o clock flight?"

"Fine Betty, really that's okay, call him back. Use my phone if you want."

Betty went out into the hall.

"But the worst of it is that I didn't decide until the day of the wedding…" Bernard looked truly unhappy with himself. "And as you may have gathered, our daughter was already on the way."

"And she still hasn't forgiven you." I blurted out.

This explained why Deirdre was so against religion, marriage, in fact anything of an institutional nature. "Sorry." I added.

"No, it's true. She won't see me; thinks the whole thing is appalling."

I didn't look at Betty. I did not want her to see my expression which clearly said, that's not the version you told me, but I could understand why.

"C'mon. Let's think about the present. Talking of which what are we going to buy the happy couple?"

Cecil got up to open the living room door as Betty seemed to be struggling from the other side.

"Here he is. I was wondering if you still had him."

Betty came in carrying a white Persian cat who leapt from her arms the moment she sat down.

"Everything ok?" Bernard asked.

"Almost," said Betty "It's just that Jean-Louis insists on bringing his best man..."

"And you want to know if he can stay here as well?"

Betty wrinkled up her nose as if trying to sense the situation.

"Well, I don't know. We *do* only have a five bedroom house..." Cecil was putting cups back on the tray as he spoke. He was much slimmer, smaller all together than Bernard. He appeared at first to have neat short dark hair until he turned and you noticed the pony tail. But he had the same depth in those brown eyes, friendly eyes.

"Of course. Who is it.?" Bernard frowned as Betty side glanced at me before answering. "Um, Paolo, his brother."

I groaned as flashbacks of overfilled champagne glasses came into view.

"I couldn't say no." Betty looked at me pleadingly.

"Is he a problem?" Cecil looked at me with amusement.

"Not for you, no." I chuckled to myself as I envisaged the scenario where maybe Paolo may be about to get a taste of 'his own medicine'.

Tuesday 19th December.

Shopping.

"Betty, have you seen the price tag?" I said a little too loudly. The exclusive Surrey boutique was not used to having their clients, comment on such things.

"Yes, I know. But, an English woman marrying a Spaniard living in France, so I thought, Betty, it's an Italian designer for you."

"But Versace!" I was turning green and wondering if maybe I should give Paolo another chance.

"When Jean-Louis said, you choose, I'll pay, what did you expect?" Betty said in her little girl voice.

Well, I didn't expect anything anymore but I couldn't help thinking, what would happen if Deirdre were to walk in here? She was probably imagining her mother having a nap before a gentle game of bridge with Audrey and her friends.

The shop door opened with a whoosh of cold air and a refined 'ding'. The changing room curtain was thrown back.

"Audrey, dahling. Glad you could come, what do you think?"

Betty kissed the air either side of her friend as she held up another shimmering revelation.

"Your daughter's been after you. She phoned half an hour ago. I said you were in the bath..."

Betty and Audrey bumped into each other as they giggled in a very unseemly fashion. I could almost see the assistant writing out a note to put the door, as we leave. Only one Audrey or one Betty in this establishment at any time.

"I apologise, how rude of me. Audrey, this is Laura, my nanny."

"How have you survived? You poor girl." Audrey squeezed my hand. "Are you buying anything?" she looked at me trying to hide the doubtful expression on her face.

For once *my* phone rang. Just your normal ring tone, but obviously enough to upset Madam shop owner. Head down I went out into a blustery bright, packed, side street. Fortunately we were at the top of the town, the signal was much better here.

"Oh okay...Do you want to open it?...That's alright, don't worry, just tell me what it says...Oh, what do you think Julia?...True, yes...is it the usual number?...ok, will do, see you later...oh by the way Jean-Louis is arriving tonight with his brother!...yes I know, thought you'd say that. Bye."

Bright it may be but it was still flipping freezing. The pavements were slippery, so most people were walking on the road. Even the side streets had been gritted. No doubt a stipulation in the latest Surrey manifesto. Much to my relief Betty and Audrey were just emerging from the designer grotto as I rounded the corner. It was twelve fifteen.

"We'd normally be thinking about lunch now wouldn't we, my little slave?"

Betty took my elbow as we almost collided in the doorway.

'Madam indoors' look of relief at our departure turned to one of anxiety as she envisaged...There's been a slight accident, could you send an ambulance, but would you park outside the Italian restaurant, there's more room there. She would probably say. But all was well and we remained upright.

"Don't tell me that was Paolo on the phone?" Betty quizzed.

"Oh, god no. It was Julia .She forgot, what with all the excitement last night, to give me a letter that had arrived from the agency."

Audrey watched, intrigued as we both fell silent. A letter from the agency meant, another job...an end to this one.

"So. We have until eight or nine this evening before the boys arrive to arrange everything. They're getting a taxi from Gatwick."

Betty's voice trailed off. She looked weary. For the first time I felt quite panicked. Audrey came to the rescue.

"Let's go and grab a bite to eat and then it's all back to my place for the afternoon."

ALL EXPENSES PAID

Tuesday 19ᵗʰ December.

Free calls.

"I'm glad you didn't move Audrey. I've always thought of this house as a second home."

Audrey was placing a large flowery patterned footstool under Betty's stockinged feet. More than I would have been allowed to do. They had been friends since school days. They shared a comfort zone that only comes with time.

I sprang up. "Right, I'd better get off to the Oxfam shop to find something for tomorrow. Any idea what time tomorrow Betty?"

"No, not yet, but when JL arrives we'll go over to Bernard's and sort it out."

"You're quite welcome to stay here till then, if you want Laura. Go and have a nap if you like."

Audrey had already said I could stay with her until after the wedding. Julia wanted me to go back with her and then there was this offer of a job, over Christmas and the New Year. Decisions, decisions.

"I'll just go and unpack first and see how I feel."

The Golden Girls nodded.

Of course I had my New Year's Eve outfit that I had bought in Cavaillon. How could I have forgotten? I had no plans for New Years Eve, but once a boy scout.

How long would Jean-Louis stay? Would they have a honeymoon? Would Paolo become all unnecessary with the romantic atmosphere? Should I take this job? The money would be useful. I must have nodded off because the sound of my phone made me jump.

"It's only me. Didn't want to wake you but we're off to The Rectory in half an hour if you want to come." Betty's voice had a strange echo to it.

"Where are you?" I asked.

"On the landing," she replied.

"Aren't you taking this, free local calls, a bit far Betty?" I said to her face as I opened my bedroom door.

"Well you don't get much for free these days do you?" She had a point. "Half an hour you say?"

Betty nodded.

"Cup of tea anyone?" Audrey's voice echoed up the large winding staircase.

"Ooh yes please Audrey. I'll be down in a minute."

Tuesday 19th December

Meet the neighbours.

Audrey's neighbour was indeed only two doors down, but in this neck of the woods, that could mean anything up to half a mile. We could have walked to The Rectory. We all agreed it was far too dark, cold and damp for that. By day the building had looked homely in a grand sort of way. Now at eight thirty on a December evening it looked like a fairytale mansion. Tiny white lights were shimmering in all the downstairs windows as if someone had gathered all the same sized stars and strung them together. Even the bay tree in the porch had a twinkle to it. A new white Mercedes was parked in front of the double garage doors.

"Oh, maybe he's got visitors." Betty delved into her handbag.

"You're not going to phone him Betty, you're becoming obsessed. Come on, he is expecting us." Audrey was taking charge, which was nice.

As Audrey was locking the car I stood behind Betty. "Are you getting cold feet?"

"Wouldn't you?" she muttered

The front door was thrown open before we had chance to ring the bell.

"Long time no see. Betty you look wonderful!" The holly wreath swayed with the jolt.

"Oh Gladys, how are you. How did you know? Is that your car?" Betty was obviously surprised by her old friend's appearance.

But before she could answer, Jean-Louis sauntered over and went down on one knee.

"Bettee," he said carefully. "Will you do me the 'onour of being my wife?"

Betty looked round. Bernard was stood in the kitchen doorway, nodding gently. Cecil was peering over his shoulder, eyes wide....waiting. Gladys pointed up towards the oak beam that crossed the hall; dangling just out of reach was a sprig of mistletoe. I was sure it hadn't been there earlier. Audrey and I held our breath.

"Cheri?" Jean-Louis was beginning to look anxious.

"Of course I will." exclaimed Betty at last "Now get up before we have to get you another new knee."

Both Cecil and Bernard turned and almost ran back into the kitchen.

"Champagne, two nights running. I could get used to this." I raised my glass to Betty who was busy catching up with Gladys.

"It will be three nights." Paolo was standing to my right. He brought his glass round to clink with mine. I frowned. "Tomorrow after the wedding, of course." He explained.

"Oh, of course. And so, how are you?" I asked, wishing I didn't have to know. There was still something about him that I couldn't put my finger on. Okay, less oil on the sleeked back hair would be nice and I didn't usually hold it against people who had a gap between their two front teeth and he obviously wasn't as fit as his brother, although he was at least ten years younger, and I had tried to like him, but no, he still made me shudder when he stood close.

"Don't worry I 'ave strict instructions. I know when I'm beaten. Betty says you 'ave someone 'ere, in England. I no wish to stand in the way." He took my right hand and kissed it lightly and backed away.

"Blimey, don't see much of that in Surrey these days." It was Julia, Cecil had just let her in. Betty had insisted that she join the party.

"You should see the dress that Betty has bought." I raised my arms and was about to go into description overdrive, when I was interrupted.

"And who is this lovely lady, may I ask?" Paolo had returned with a glass of champagne for Julia. "Do you have someone 'ere too?"

"You must be Paolo." Julia quipped, struggling not to look at me.

"You 'ave 'eard about me?" he preened.

"Oh indeed I have. Laura has told me heaps about you."

"'eaps, what is this 'eaps?"

"I don't suppose you know anything about espresso machines, do you Paolo?" Cecil had placed his left hand on Paolo's broad back. "It's just that I can't seem to get a really good head ..."

Julia blew bubbles into her champagne. You could see Paolo looking very puzzled at such behaviour, as he was led away into the Gaggeneau fairyland. Betty was chatting nineteen to the dozen, whilst Audrey and Gladys were in rapt attention. Jean-Louis was having a guided tour of the photos on the piano.

Paolo and Cecil could be seen through the open kitchen door, heads bobbing in unison. "Yes, that's it. It's the rhythm. It is important."

"What a party." Julia looked at me. "You don't want to leave do you?"

I shook my head. For once words failed me. I felt a lump of sadness gathering in my throat, stinging the back of my eyes. I was so happy for Betty but I didn't want her to go. Julia knew better than to be sympathetic, a sure way to start the waterworks.

"So, did you phone about that job? Are you going to take it or do I have to put up with you all Christmas, going on about 'in France this and in France that," she mocked, wanting to say the right thing.

I swallowed hard and thought about how Bette Davis would handle the situation.

"You're right I must take the job. I cannot wallow in self pity. Reminiscing only gets in the way of the future." I completed the sentence with a bow, almost colliding with Bernard's knee caps on the way up.

"Are you okay my dear?" Bernard asked me but was looking at Julia for confirmation.

"You can see why they got on so well can't you." Julia warmed to the man of the cloth. "Are you glad you chose the church?"

"Me?" Bernard wasn't sure exactly what Julia meant. "Oh, you mean instead of love?" he said looking across at Betty.

"Julia! Isn't that a bit...well... personal?" I admonished.

"Ah no, it's okay," Bernard reassured us. "It wasn't really a choice in the end. Some things aren't, are they?"

Cecil had appeared at his side with a stainless steel jug brimming with foaming hot milk.

"Some things aren't what Bernie? How much champagne have you had?"

He raised his eyebrows at me and Julia before scooping a dollop of froth from the jug and placing it squarely on the end of Bernard's bulbous nose.

"Um oh, Bernard...I ...well...really must be off." Gladys was looking very uncomfortable, not knowing where to look. She did wish that they didn't have to behave like this. It wasn't normal. Bernard was such a nice man. Her Harold didn't approve at all. Don't be long he'd said. She was only allowed to come because Betty was here. She didn't dare mention Jean-Louis.

An 82 yr old English woman marrying a 69 yr old Spanish mechanic (he would say) garage owner (Gladys would correct him).

"Let me see you home." Bernard was walking towards the door and wiping the offending froth from his nose.

"No really Bernard, you're very kind but I prefer to walk alone." She raised her hand and was gone.

Probably the only chance she gets, thought Bernard. That Harold seemed to have her on a pretty tight leash.

"So what was the mission, should you decide to take it, set by the agency?" Betty had been catching up recently on all the 80's American shows on the daytime M6 channel. "Where is it, the job I mean?"

"Not far really. In fact back the way we came, a little village just next door to Rutherfield." I surveyed Betty's eyes for a reaction.

"Oh well then you'd have Sasha for company if things get bad," Betty said, but I could tell her mind was elsewhere. And why shouldn't it be, this time tomorrow she would be Mrs or should that be Madam JL Camillo. They had ordered the cake and the flowers over the phone. Gladys worked part time in the local bakers. Patisserie, Harold called it. And not surprisingly Bernard had one or two contacts in the floristry business. I can do the photographs, Cecil had offered.

"So, when do you start?" Betty smiled at me.

"They want me to go tomorrow."

"Oh, well. If you have to..." Betty bit her lip as she tried to think what to say.

"And I said I couldn't get there until the day after!"

Betty threw her arms around me. "Are you sure?"

"It should suit old Scrooge here, down to the ground." Julia joined in the conversation.

"Why, what do you mean?" Betty queried.

"Oh hasn't she told you; it's assistant housekeeper to a wealthy Muslim family."

"But I thought they didn't celebrate..."

"Exactly."

Julia laughed.

"Different?" I suggested, more in fear than in hope.

"Gather round folks. Jean-Louis has an announcement to make." Bernard was tapping the side of his champagne glass with the sharp end of the letter opener.

"Another one?" I looked at Betty.

She was obviously just as surprised. Her usual shrug was hesitant, tinged with anticipation. He beckoned his brother towards him as he spoke.

"As you all know from tomorrow my life will change."

The room fell silent; only the cat was preoccupied rearranging the fringe on the edge of the Persian rug. I wondered if they might be related.

"For the better," he continued, as we all nodded. "And time is, well, precious." He seemed to be struggling with whatever he was about to say. "Some say it will never happen, but Bettee, she is special non?" The communal nodding continued. "And so, it is with great pride and love, that from today I 'and over the running of my garage to my brother Paolo."

He shuddered as he heard himself say the words. He had sworn he'd never retire. No-one moved. The cat stopped scrabbling and rolled onto its back. Paolo moved to stand next to his brother. Still no-one said anything, until Betty broke the spell.

"Oh my God, you mean I've got to put up with you twenty four hours a day."

Jean-Louis feigned a wounded look. Paolo enveloped his brother in a bear hug. Cecil wiped away a single tear. "You 'ave. And it starts with our 'oneymoon!"

"See, I told you he would have arranged something," I whispered to Betty.

"Honeymoon?" was all Betty could manage.

"You remember we 'ave a villa in Marrakech?"

Betty looked on edge. She had visions of being greeted by the whole family.

"And no-one goes there until New Year's Eve," he adds, as if reading her doubts. "So we can have almost a week to ourselves. Our usual housekeeper is not there but we can eat out every day. I think we can manage. What do you say?" he turned to Betty, who had sat down on the poufee with her back leaning against the piano. The cat had sidled over for some attention.

"Will someone pinch me?" Betty asked looking around the room at the assembled smiling faces.

"Not necessary Cheri. I promise."

Cecil whimpered and had to excuse himself. Julia gave me a hug. Audrey came and stood by Betty putting her arm around her shoulder.

"You don't really need a wedding ceremony, do you?" Bernard glanced from Betty to Jean-Louis. "Your eyes say it all. Now I don't want to be a party pooper but don't you think we should call it a day. After all we still have a few things to do before tomorrow. And the bride should get her beauty sleep."

"Cheek," said Betty lifting her chin and stroking her neck. Jean-Louis took her hand and held it in his as he leant over to whisper something in her ear.

Tuesday 19th December.

And Finally.

"What an evening Betty. You were surprised to see, what was her name?"

"Gladys." Betty volunteered.

"Oh yes. But not like you and Audrey is she?"

I decided I had probably said enough, as I glanced at Betty, her eyes were closing.

"Night, Laura. Sweet dreams." Betty rolled over onto her right side so that I could only see the back of her head.

"Oh Laura, I forgot to ask. I couldn't get an appointment at my old local hairdresser for tomorrow, would you mind doing my hair for me?"

"Of course I don't mind. Goodnight."

I switched off the main light with the braided pulley behind the headboard.

Dreams. I'd be lucky. I did not know how Betty did it. How could she sleep with all that was going on? And I still felt guilty that I was enjoying all this and Deirdre and Gerard didn't even know any of it. She had looked stunning in the pale turquoise sequined dress. JL was going to cry I felt sure. Talk about better late than never. Not the marrying kind; always lived for his work and his racing. He had everything he wanted. That was what Paolo had told me that evening.

So much had happened...

Still, a wealthy Muslim family that had all its food delivered from Harrods should be interesting. How would the rest of JL's family take to Betty? She wasn't your average octogenarian. She had become an instant step grandmother, she would like that.

There was a gentle tap on the door; either that or my head was finally coming lose.

"Hello?" I called out quietly.

"Laura it's me Audrey, are you both awake?"

I had to laugh. Who else could it be, seeing as Audrey lived alone?

"Well I am. Is something wrong?" I asked.

The door opened slowly and Audrey appeared in a quilted pink dressing gown and two pink sponge rollers on top of her head.

"No nothing's wrong." she hissed.

"Good grief, you two, a girl *does* need some beauty sleep." Betty snapped on her bedside lamp.

"Sorry, but I thought you'd like to know...this news...um...now," Audrey had a distinct look of superiority about her. "There was a message on my answer phone when we got back and I've only just remembered to listen to it..."

We turned to look at Audrey. "Well she said it was okay for me to tell you, so I will," she said.

"Preferably before I die, Audrey."

Betty pulled herself up to a sitting position.

"It's Deirdre."

I saw Betty's face tighten.

"She says to tell you she's pregnant."

"Good grief," was Betty's reply.

"She said she couldn't be sure before you left or she would have told you herself," Audrey added.

"Ah," was all Betty could manage.

"Goodness me, I've never known so much happen in such a short time."

My head was spinning.

"Really? Well, seeing as we're all now wide awake why don't I give you something else to think about." Betty gave a tired but satisfied sigh.

"There's more?" I enquired.

"There can't be."Audrey suggested, sitting down on the edge of my bed.

"Well, you heard JL say he was going to give up work when we get back to France. Well he also wants us to take a few trips, and you know how lonely *his* house would get with no-one in it. He doesn't have a *housekeeper*... and when we *are* there we could always use a bit of pampering..."

Audrey poked me in the ribs as I didn't seem to be getting the message.

Betty tossed my phone to me.

I hit speedial.

"Julia, I know it's late. I'm sorry but you'll never guess... fantastic news..."

******

Cecil drove Betty in her wonderful old cream and burgundy Alfa Romeo to the church. JL cried when he saw it. Bernard had been keeping it in his garage. Cecil gave Betty away.

Betty and Jean-Louis became Mr and Mrs Camillo on Wednesday 2oth December at midday. Not a dry eye in the place. Audrey mentioned the bans not being read. Bernard and Betty just shrugged.

I went off to the Hussein family for two weeks as planned. Then I flew to Marseille to take up my new post as resident housekeeper to the newlyweds.

Betty and Jean-Louis flew to Marrakech via Marseille to see Deirdre and Gerard.

Deirdre and Gerard insisted that Betty and Jean-Louis return in time for their party on New Year's Eve and told Betty that her grandchild's ETA was 13th May. Betty's birthday.

Note from the author.

All Expenses Paid was written as a one off.

However, as I get to the end of editing, I know I am going to miss Betty too much. All Expenses Paid is set in the summer of 1995.

Outlines for the next seventeen novels taking us to 2012 are in place.

For example:

Betty with Graham Norton in 2007.

Betty on Gok in 2008.

Betty with Betty White on SNL in 2010.

Also by Helen Ducal.

Available on Amazon.com and co.uk

A Mouse in the Vinaigrette. Twenty six short stories, based on the real tales of a live-in carer.

Khamaileon. A maternity suit and even DNA cannot help her.

Shelf Life. EveryBody has one. Would you want to know yours?

Coming soon.

Mature, educated, healing hands, can travel. An erotic memoir.

Works In Progress.

Novels:

Wait for Me. Two souls, six lives. 1860's India.1920's Austria. 2000 UK.

Decree Absolutely. You keep the house (and develop a thriving business)

Stage plays:

Souvenir. A play without words. Music from 1950's to 1990's, tell the story.

Parallel Lives. Two Iconoclasts tell 'their' story. Colette and Madonna.

TV Drama.

Not Always. Abuse begets abuse...Not Always.

A Knock at the door. Treated for the 'wrong' complaint.

Philosophy: The only life worth living is the one you create for yourself.

I was determined to be a writer ever since being asked to leave the Brownies for chalking on the benches. Had my first business at 19, married at 20, divorced at 30, ditched the 9-5 at 40 to work as a live-in carer, working in Europe, travelling to Australia and writing in between. Got a first in Media Writing (BA Hons) at 50, moved to France, where I recharge my batteries, write, eat and sleep. But still have to return to Blighty every 2 weeks to earn my rent, until I can write full time.

Contact the author: www.helenducal.com

Or find her on Facebook https://www.facebook.com/helen.ducal

And twitter. @khamaileon

Helen Ducal

Printed in Great Britain
by Amazon